Teletext and Viewdata

Steve A Money

T.Eng(CEI), MBCS, MITE

Newnes Technical Books

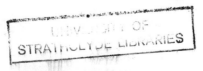

The Butterworth Group

United Kingdom	Butterworth & Co (Publishers) Ltd London: 88 Kingsway, WC2B 6AB
Australia	Butterworths Pty Ltd Sydney: 586 Pacific Highway, Chatswood, NSW 2067 Also at Melbourne, Brisbane, Adelaide and Perth
Canada	Butterworth & Co (Canada) Ltd Toronto: 2265 Midland Avenue, Scarborough, Ontario, M1P 4S1
New Zealand	Butterworths of New Zealand Ltd Wellington: T & W Young Building, 77—85 Customhouse Quay, 1, CPO Box 472
South Africa	Butterworth & Co (South Africa) (Pty) Ltd Durban: 152—154 Gale Street
USA	Butterworth (Publishers) Inc Boston: 10 Tower Office Park, Woburn, Mass. 01801

First published 1979 by Newnes Technical Books
a Butterworth imprint

© Butterworth & Co (Publishers) Ltd, 1979

British Library Cataloguing in Publication Data

Money, Steve A
    Teletext and viewdata.
    1. Teletext and viewdata.
    2. Viewdata (Data transmission system)
    I. Title
    621.388   TK5105   79-40496

    ISBN 0-408-00378-2

Typeset by Butterworths Litho Preparation Department
Printed in England by Fakenham Press Ltd., Fakenham, Norfolk

D
621 . 388
MoN

Preface

In recent years the role of the domestic television receiver has begun to change. Whereas in the past the TV set was used solely for viewing broadcast programmes today it can be used as a display for a video game or, perhaps, to present pages of written text information from services such as teletext and viewdata. Microprocessor-based personal computer systems may also use TV receives to display text or graphics information.

These new applications of the television receiver make use of a series of digital electronic techniques which may be unfamiliar to the reader. My aim in this book has been to explain, in simple terms, the principles of operation of the teletext and viewdata systems and to describe the various electronic techniques employed to decode the data signals and to produce a display of text on the television screen. Many of the commercial decoder modules which are available in the UK and other countries are examined and their operating principles are fully explained.

I am greatly indebted to the following organisations for their invaluable help in providing information and some of the photographs in the preparation of this book:

British Broadcasting Corporation.
Independent Television Authority.
British Post Office.
Texas Instruments Ltd.
General Instrument Microelectronics Ltd.
G.E.C. Ltd.
Mullard Ltd.
Intel Semiconductors Corp.
Thorn Consumer Electronics Ltd.
ITT Consumer Products Ltd.

Steve Money

Contents

Chapter 1

Introduction

In ancient Greece the priests seeking information, usually about the future, would go to Delphi and consult the Oracle of Zeus. Today the television viewer in Britain might also consult ORACLE in search of information. Unlike the Greeks however our modern viewer is not enlisting the help of the Gods but merely using one version of a totally new concept in broadcasting services, called teletext. This began full-scale operations in the UK in the autumn of 1976, after a lengthy series of test transmissions. The USA and other countries also provide text information services for their TV viewers mainly based on the British system.

Developed by engineers of the British Broadcasting Corporation (BBC) and Independent Broadcasting Authority (IBA) during the early 1970s the teletext system allows viewers to call up, in place of the normal television picture, a display of some hundreds of different pages of text information on a wide range of topics. The data signals for teletext are transmitted as part of the normal television signal but are not usually visible to the ordinary television viewer. In order to see the teletext service a specially adapted television receiver is required which will decode the teletext signals and display the corresponding pages of text information on the screen in place of the programme picture.

Using teletext and viewdata

Let us now look at teletext in action. We will suppose that our viewer has just arrived home from work and that he wants to find out which horse won the 15.30 race. This information is not normally included in the television newscast so he might have to go out and buy a newspaper or perhaps even wait until the following day to read the results in a newspaper. But our viewer wants to know the result immediately and this is where teletext comes into use.

Switching on the television our viewer might tune to BBC1 and then select the teletext mode. It is assumed that his receiver is designed to receive the teletext service. Using the teletext control unit, which may be a keyboard like that on a pocket calculator, he selects page 100 and within a few seconds the main index page for the BBC Ceefax service will appear on the screen as shown in *Figure 1.1*. Next he selects page

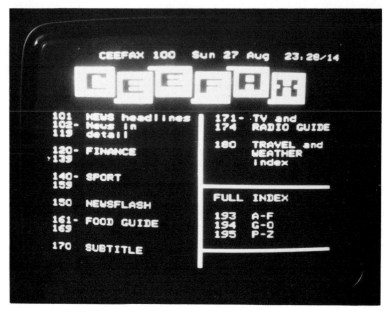

Figure 1.1   Ceefax title page (P100)

140 for the sports index in order to find out the page number for the racing results. Finally he dials up the appropriate page number and results appear on the screen as shown in *Figure 1.2*. All of this activity will have taken just a few minutes. Of course our viewer might equally well have selected the local ITV channel and used their Oracle service to obtain the same information.

If our viewer is not a racing person he (or she) might have selected some of the other 150 to 200 different pages of information that would be available on each television channel. These would cover national and international news, sports, finance, entertainment, weather, travel information, recipes and a multitude of other items that might be of interest. There is even a horoscope page on Oracle — so maybe this service is not so much different from the ancient Oracle of Zeus after all! The electronic newspaper has finally become a reality. With a teletext receiver we have available, at the touch of a button, a wealth of up to the minute information.

Apart from teletext however another information service is also available to our viewer. Here the data signals are sent over the telephone line but the information is displayed on television in the same way as

Figure 1.2   Teletext racing results page

for teletext. This alternative information system is called 'viewdata' and provides an even greater range of information than the broadcast teletext services.

Before going on to look at the technical aspects of these new services it might be interesting to see how they developed over the years.

From morse to teleprinters

The idea of some sort of electronic newspaper has been thought about since the early days of radio but it was not until the early 1970s and the development of the teletext and viewdata systems that it could become a practical reality.

In the early days radio was primarily used for communication and for providing news and weather information. Signals were transmitted using the dots and dashes of the Morse code and skilled operators would translate these into written messages. Sometimes the dots and dashes might be printed out on a narrow strip of paper to give a permanent record.

It was a logical step to arrange that letters and numbers could be printed out on the paper strip instead of the Morse dots and dashes. A different form of coding, known as the Baudot code, was used for this purpose and the well known 'ticker tape' machines of the 1920s were the result. This type of message transmission was used for sending telegrams and providing information to the Stock Exchange and is still used occasionally today.

The 'ticker tape' system was quite effective but had the disadvantage that if you wanted the information in page form the strips of paper had to be cut up and pasted on to a sheet of paper. To overcome this problem page printers were developed. These look very much like a typewriter except that they are electrically operated and will print out the text in page format on a roll of paper. Teleprinter machines such as these are widely used today for commercial applications and by the news agencies.

Unfortunately teleprinter machines are bulky and very expensive so they were not particularly suited for providing a domestic information service. Another problem with this mode of transmission however is that it is quite slow and the receiving station has little or no control over the information being received. All the information being sent has to be received in order to get the piece you actually need. With their complex mechanical systems such machines as teleprinters need to be regularly maintained which makes them rather unsuited for use in the normal home environment.

Text on television

By the 1930s radio was being used primarily as an entertainment medium although news bulletins were included at certain periods in the day's programmes. At this time television was still in its infancy and was seen only by rather limited audiences.

It was not until the mid 1960s that television had almost spread to the point where virtually every household had at least one television receiver. It now became a possibility that the television receiver itself might be used as a replacement for the expensive teleprinter, and text information presented as a picture on the screen.

A simple way of implementing such an information system would be to present the text in much the same way as the titles of a normal television programme where a camera is set up to take a picture of the page of text. This arrangement, however, requires one or more television channels to be allocated solely for text transmission. In fact this technique is widely used by cable television networks in the USA and Canada where one channel is set aside for a text information service.

In these cable television systems the screen display for the text service consists of eight to twelve lines of text as shown in *Figure 1.3*.

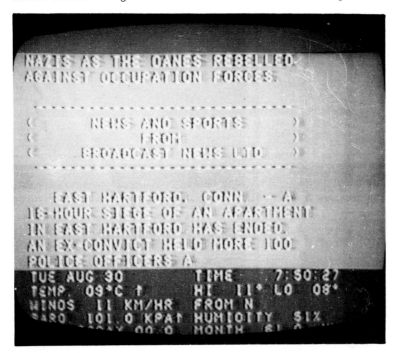

Figure 1.3   Typical page from Canadian Cable TV news

The text is moved up the TV screen one line at a time at a rate of about one line every two or three seconds. As one line moves off the top of the display a new line replaces it at the bottom to give the effect of a roll of printed text being slowly drawn past the screen.

A typical bulletin on these cable television news broadcasts might take about half an hour to be displayed and then the whole process would start again at the beginning of the text. This type of display does have a certain fascination for the viewer since he is always waiting to see what the next line of text or news item is going to be. However it can also be a bit tedious if the item you want to see is near the end of the bulletin and you have to sit through the rest of the news even though you are not interested in it. This is fundamentally the same problem that existed with the teleprinter system.

Apart from the rolling text display, parts of the picture area may be used for fixed text displays giving information such as the time, local weather and perhaps the traffic conditions. Often these parts of the display are presented in a different colour from the main text. The sound channel for the text transmission is usually a continuous music broadcast.

Whilst the allocation of a channel solely to text is acceptable on a cable television network it is not at all popular for broadcast television where the number of available channels is limited and usually all of the channels are needed to provide a normal television service.

Flashing dots and subcarrier systems

If a separate channel cannot be allocated to a text transmission is it possible to send the text data using the same channel as the normal picture and sound signals?

One idea proposed in the USA was to use a flashing dot tucked away in the corner of the screen to carry the text data signals. At the receiving end, a photocell was mounted in front of the screen to detect the signals from the flashing dot and these were used to drive some form of teleprinter machine to produce printed text.

For colour television a sub-carrier signal located at the high end of the video channel is used to carry the colour information whilst the sound signal is also carried on a second sub-carrier signal. It seems possible therefore to use a sub-carrier to carry the text information.

In 1973 the Hazeltine Corporation in the USA did in fact propose such a scheme using a sub-carrier in the region of 2 to 3 MHz which carried a text data signal at the rate of some 21 000 bits per second. Here the display of text was produced by using a special character generator system within the TV set to convert the data signals into a television picture.

Although some experiments were carried out using both of these techniques nothing much seems to have happened since they were proposed.

Using blank lines

In the 625-line system only about 575 of the scan lines are actually used to form the picture on the screen. About eight lines are used for vertical synchronisation whilst the remainder are blanked to allow the scanning beams at the camera and receiver to carry out the vertical retrace at the end of each field scan.

Engineers looked at these blank scan lines and tried to think of some way in which they might be used. The first possibility was to use them to carry test signals. As the programmes increased to fill most of the available air time there were fewer opportunities to transmit test cards for the alignment of transmitters and receivers.

Eventually these test signals were inserted into one or two of the blank lines at the top of the picture. Here one scan line might carry a grey scale pattern whilst a second might be used for a bandwidth test signal. Later colour test signals were included to produce a colour bar pattern on one of the normally blank scan lines. Viewers would not normally be aware of these signals since they would be displayed just off the top edge of the screen if the receiver were properly adjusted. Today two scan lines are regularly used for test signals so that engineers can check the performance of the television system whilst the programmes are being transmitted.

The next logical step was to send some form of data signal on these blank lines. This was particularly useful to the engineers of the independent television network (ITV) in the UK where several different companies generate the programmes and good communication was needed between the various programme centres in the network and the television transmitters which are run by the Independent Broadcasting Authority (IBA). Soon a system known as SLICE (Source Labelling Indication and Control Equipment) had been developed. This system used data which was inserted into lines 16 and 328 on alternate field scans.

These data signals would identify the source of the accompanying picture, provide status information about the network and might also include simple messages. A similar system was also being used by the BBC and today a Slice transmission is regularly used for communication between various stations in the European television network.

Ceefax and Oracle

If data signals could be sent around the network on blank scan lines then they could equally well be used to send messages to ordinary television viewers and it was thought that a system like Slice might be used to transmit subtitles to some viewers without including them in the normal programme picture. It was only a small step from this idea to the possibility of transmitting a magazine consisting of several pages of text and allowing the TV viewer to select the page he wanted to display. Thus the basic idea for the teletext service was born.

In America, RCA proposed a system which they called Homefax where data signals were sent on blank lines and used at the receiving end to drive an electrographic type printer to produce a printed page of text. However this was really only another development of the teleprinter type systems.

The main drive towards a public text information service via television was to develop in the UK where engineers at both the BBC and IBA started work on rival schemes for such a service. By the end of 1972 both groups had devised experimental proposals for such a service.

By April 1973 the system developed by IBA engineers and called Oracle started test transmissions from the ITV transmitter at Crystal Palace, London. Using the same basic data system as Slice the text signals were carried on one blank line in each field scan. The name Oracle (Optional Reception of Announcements by Coded Line Electronics) was perhaps an apt choice for this new experimental service since the original Oracle at Delphi had been a source of information which could be consulted as required.

For these test transmissions about 50 different pages of information were transmitted and the viewer was able to select any one of them and display it on his screen. A page consisted of 22 lines of text with 40 characters in each line and the pages were transmitted continuously at a rate of just over one second. At first only the capital letters and figures were provided and the display was in black and whire. For later transmissions lower case symbols, graphics patterns and colour were added. The information presented was a sample of what a real magazine might be like and consisted of news, sports, finance, entertainment and general interest items which were updated from time to time.

Meanwhile the BBC had developed their Teledata system and were to start test transmissions soon after the Oracle tests began. The name of the BBC service was later changed to Ceefax (See Facts) and it provided about 32 pages of text with a format of 24 rows and 32 characters per row. Because they used a higher data rate and two blank lines for Ceefax the BBC transmitted pages at about two per second giving a faster access time to display a selected page.

Unified teletext standard

During these early test transmissions the decoders used to receive and display the pages of text had been complicated by the need to deal with two different systems. Whilst it was very soon demonstrated that a public text information service was perfectly feasible it was obvious that some common standard for the transmissions was needed. Engineers from the BBC and IBA now formed a committee with representatives of the television industry to devise a unified standard for text transmission.

The best features of each of the original systems were incorporated and the whole system was expanded to cater for possible future developments. By January 1974 a new common standard had been worked out and the service was given the general name 'teletext'.

This new standard allowed for selection of up to 800 different pages on a single channel and the transmission rate was increased to four pages a second. A page now had 24 rows of 40 characters each and provision was made for colour, graphics and time coded pages.

Figure 1.4   Off screen picture showing teletext data

By the middle of 1974 transmissions using the new standard had begun in earnest and although the BBC and ITV services retained their old names of Ceefax and Oracle they were technically identical. Magazine sizes increased to a hundred or more pages and experiments began with the techniques of editing a teletext magazine. Meanwhile a series of transmission tests over the networks was started to see how the data signals fared in various conditions.

Soon many of the transmitters around the country were radiating teletext signals as well as normal television programmes. In fact the service was virtually operational but there were relatively few receivers that could decode the signals for the new service.

Teletext in Europe

Whilst teletext worked very well on the British 625 line TV standard where the video bandwidth was 5.5 MHz, would it work in Europe where a bandwidth of only 5 MHz was used? Test transmissions were carried out in Sweden and Germany using both v.h.f. and u.h.f. transmissions to see how teletext would work. The results were highly successful and showed that the British teletext standard could easily be adopted for both the European and International 625 line television standards.

Teletext might also be adapted for use on the 525 line 60 fields per second system used in the USA and a number of other countries. Here the number of rows of text in a page would be reduced to 20 and data for each row would be contained in two successive blank lines.

In 1976, in the UK the unified standard was slightly altered to add more facilities and then the two services began operations in earnest to build up a public service.

Viewdata

Whilst teletext was being developed the British Post Office was also working on a scheme for providing a public text information service. Here the text data would be sent to the user via the ordinary public

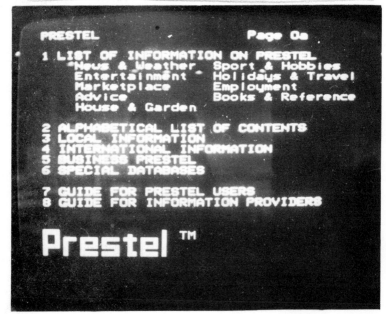

Figure 1.5   Main index page from Prestel service

telephone network. He would simply dial the number of the new service and would be connected to a computer system which would then transmit data for a selected page along the phone line (*Figure 1.5*). This system was called 'viewdata'. In 1978 the system became available experimentally in Britain and the Post Office renamed their system Prestel (see chapter 10).

With the development of teletext the logical step was to make the viewdata and teletext standards compatible so that the television receiver could also be used to show pages of text from the viewdata system.

Unlike teletext, the viewdata system allows for more interaction with the user. Having been connected to the viewdata computer centre the viewer will gain access to a vast data bank controlled by the computer and may be able to select from hundreds of thousands of different pages of text. In this case only the requested page need be sent along the telephone line so the data rate can be much lower. Apart from selecting a page however the user can also send his own messages to the computer and may even be able to use the computer system itself when his viewdata unit will be a remote terminal for the computer system.

Users might be charged a fee for selecting some of the pages of information in much the same way as they are charged for phone calls.

Other systems

Recently two text transmissions systems have been developed in France. One called Antiope is in many ways a similar system to teletext although rather more complex in its operation. It can be broadcast together with a television signal in the same way as teletext.

The second French system is called Tictac and seems to be a simplified version of the British viewdata system using the normal telephone network as a transmission medium.

A viewdata system which is currently undergoing field trials is the Canadian Telidon system. This is claimed to be more advanced than any existing system.

Technical aspects of teletext

Modern teletext decoders have only become possible because of the advances in semiconductor and integrated circuit technology in recent years. They make use of a wide range of digital logic techniques which may be rather unfamiliar to the ordinary television engineer and in this book some of these techniques and their application in a teletext decoder will be explained.

Chapter 2

The Teletext Signal

In a television channel the video signal has an instantaneous voltage level which is directly proportional to the brightness of the picture element being scanned at that instant in time. This type of signal is known as an analogue signal. Both the sound and colour components are also analogue in form since in both cases the voltage is proportional to the parameter that it represents.

A teletext data signal however is not an analogue signal and obeys a completely different set of rules. It is in fact a digital signal. Since the teletext system makes extensive use of digital signals and techniques it might be as well to take a look at some of the various concepts and the terminology associated with such systems.

Digital signals

Unlike the more familiar analogue signals which may take up, within certain limits, an infinite variety of voltage levels a digital signal can normally take up only one of two signal levels. Digital systems effectively work on a switching principle where the signals are 'on' or 'off' with no intermediate states.

The 'off' condition is generally referred to as a 'zero' or '0' state and usually, but not always, this is represented by zero volts. On the other hand the 'on' signal condition is called the 'one' or '1' state and in the majority of logic systems this is represented by a positive voltage of some four to five volts.

Other names may sometimes be used to describe these two digital signal states. For instance the '0' state may be referred to as 'low' or 'false' whilst the corresponding names for the '1' state would be 'high' or 'true'. In this book the '0' and '1' terminology will be used to describe logic signal states.

As an example of a digital system we might consider the simple circuit of *Figure 2.1* consisting of an electric lamp in series with a switch and a battery. When the switch is closed the circuit is complete and the lamp lights. The lamp can now be said to be in the '1' state. If the switch is opened current ceases to flow and the lamp goes out to leave it in the '0' state. Even if a more powerful lamp is used it will still be either on or off although its light output in the on state may be greater.

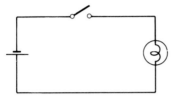

Figure 2.1   Simple logic circuit using a lamp and switch showing basic on/off conditions

In a logic circuit the actual voltage that represents a '1' state need not have an exact value. In a typical digital logic system any voltage above say +2.5 volts is considered to be a '1' level whilst voltages below +2.5 volts might be treated as '0' conditions. This property of a '0' or '1' state having a range of possible values is quite common in digital systems and may have to be taken into account when the system is designed.

Binary signals

So far the digital signals discussed have assumed a binary or two state system with signal levels of '1' or '0'. In fact a three state (ternary) system using levels of +1, −1 and 0 could be used and quaternary (four level) or even decimal (10 level) systems are also possible. In practice such systems are rarely used and virtually all of the logic schemes use the binary system.

In order to convey text information a large number of different signals are needed to represent the various letters, numbers and signs of the text message. A binary logic signal however can convey only the states 0 and 1. This situation can be overcome by using the pattern of logic states of a number of independent binary signals on separate wires to represent the individual text symbols.

Suppose there are two binary signals on separate wires. There can be four possible combinations of logic states produced on the two wires. These are 00, 01, 10 and 11 where the pair of digits shows the logic state of the pair of signals for each combination. If three separate signals are used the number of possible patterns goes up to eight. For four signals sixteen combinations occur and so on. The number of possible patterns will double for each additional signal.

When there are three signals making up the pattern the eight combinations produced can be used to represent the numbers 0 to 7 and will be written 000 to 111. Each of the digits in these numbers may now be given a weight value. In the decimal system the digits are given weight values of units, tens, hundreds, thousands, etc. For binary numbers the weights of the digits are units, twos, fours, eights etc. Thus the decimal number 13 would be written as 1101 in the binary system. This can be broken down as follows,

$$1101 = (1 \times 8) + (1 \times 4) + (0 \times 2) + (1 \times 1) = 13$$

Bits, bytes and words

The pattern of 0 and 1 states used to represent data, such as a text symbol, is called a data word or simply a *Word*. Thus the binary pattern 1101 is an example of a word. Each of the logic states or digits in the binary word is called a *Bit* so the pattern 101101 will be a six bit data word. In fact words can contain any number of bits we like to choose. The more bits there are in a word the greater the number of different words there can be.

In teletext, twenty-five different word patterns are needed to represent the letters of the alphabet plus a further ten for figures giving a minimum of thirty-five different data words. A five bit data word allows only thirty-two possible combinations so teletext must use at least six bits in the data word. To accommodate lower case letters and punctuation signs some ninety-six different words are required and this implies the use of a seven bit data word.

Eight bit words are often used in digital computers and this particular word size has been given the special name *Byte*. For convenience the teletext system uses these eight bit bytes with seven bits conveying the text data and the remaining bit used for error checks.

Serial data

So far the individual logic signals making up the data word have been assumed to be on separate wires giving a parallel presentation of the bits of the data word. Teletext, viewdata and many other data transmission systems are however limited to only one wire, or channel, along which the data signals must be conveyed. This situation is resolved by using serial transmission where the individual bits of the data words are sent one after another in time.

A typical example of a serial transmission is Morse code. Here the patterns of dots and dashes representing the symbols of the message are transmitted one after the other. The dots may be considered as logic 0 bits whilst dashes are bits at logic 1 and each set of dots and dashes is a data word representing one of the letters or numbers in the message.

In Morse code the number of dots and dashes used to represent a letter may vary from one to five so the word length varies from word to word in the message. This is not very convenient for an automatic transmission so in teletext the word length is made constant at eight bits per word.

Asynchronous transmission

In Morse transmission the differentiation between the 1 and 0 bits is achieved by making the 1 pulses (dashes) longer in time than the 0 pulses (dots). Between each of the pulses a short period of no signal is used to separate the individual bits. For data transmission this is a rather inefficient technique and the normal method used to transmit data is to allocate equal time slots to all of the data bits and to use one voltage level to represent 1 and a second level for 0.

In Morse transmission the individual code groups for the letters of the message are separated by space periods rather longer than those between adjacent dots and dashes in a symbol code, as shown in *Figure 2.2*. For serial data transmission a similar technique may be used as

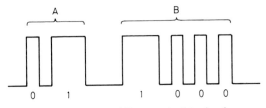

Figure 2.2   Typical Morse code data signals

shown in *Figure 2.3*. Here each symbol is represented by a 10 or 11 bit data sequence of which eight bits convey the message and the remaining bits are used to provide synchronisation between the transmitter and receiver systems.

In data transmission terminology the 1 logic state of the signal is usually called a *Mark* whilst the 0 state is called a *Space*. When no data is being transmitted the transmitter will send a continuous mark signal and the receiver system idles. At the beginning of every symbol sequence a Space bit is sent during the first bit period. This is called the *Start* bit and signals to the receiver that a data word is about to be sent. The following eight bits convey the data for the symbol then, at the end of the data sequence, one or two bits at the Mark level are sent. These are called the *Stop* bits.

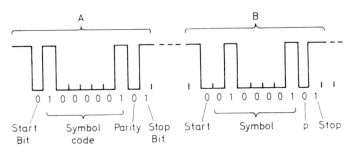

Figure 2.3   Asynchronous start/stop coding as used for viewdata signals

Often data for this type of transmission will be produced by an operator using a typewriter style keyboard. Each time a key is pressed the appropriate code is sent. The data rate is usually rather higher than the typing speed of the operator so there will be periods of Mark signals between the symbols whilst the operator searches for the next key to press. At the receiver the decoding circuits are synchronised at the start of each data word by detecting the mark to space transition of the *Start* bit. Because the receiver and transmitter systems are pulled into synchronism only when a data word is transmitted this form of transmission is usually called Asynchronous *Start Stop*.

When a human operator sends data on this type of system the reception of data words may be rather erratic since it will depend upon the rate at which the operator presses the keys. For automatic transmission the data words will follow one another in sequence with no gaps to give the maximum transmission rate. Here the Stop bits at the end of each word group provide the separation signals needed by the receiver. After each Stop bit the receiver looks for the Mark to Space transition of the following Start bit to detect the beginning of the next data word.

The *Start/Stop* mode of transmission is used for the signals in viewdata where the data is sent over a normal telephone circuit. This mode of transmission is also used for teleprinter links and for communication with computers.

In serial data systems the rate at which the data signal is sent is usually quoted in either bits per second or Baud. Typically a teleprinter system might use 110 or 300 bits per second since speed is limited by the rate at which the printer can operate. Other systems where data may be displayed on a television style display can use data rates up to 9600 bits per second. For most purposes the Baud rate is the same as bits per second so 100 baud is 100 bits/sec.

Data signals for transmission over a telephone line are often converted into tone signals with one tone for a *Mark* and a second tone for a *Space*. Special units at each end of the line convert tones to logic and vice versa.

Synchronous transmission

The Asychronous Start/Stop method of transmission is primarily designed to cope with the irregular data rates produced by human operators and has the disadvantage that two or three bits of each data word are used for the Start and Stop synchronisation signals. For high-speed automatic transmission these extra bits tend to be superfluous and it is convenient to eliminate them. This can be done by sending the eight bit symbol codes one after another as shown in *Figure 2.4*. Now data for a complete row of text may be sent as a single continuous block of data pulses.

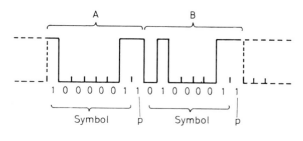

p = Parity Bit

Figure 2.4   Synchronous transmission as used in teletext and showing symbols A & B in data stream

In order to decode the incoming data some means of synchronising the receiver and transmitter systems must be provided. Instead of carrying out synchronisation at each symbol code, as in the Start/Stop system, a burst of synchronisation signals is now provided at the start of the block of data and the receiver circuits must be so designed that once synchronisation is established it can be maintained throughout the rest of the data block. This technique is called Synchronous Data Transmission.

Synchronisation is carried out in two stages. First, a burst of pulses is sent to enable the receiver timing circuits to adjust to the data rate of the received signal; second, a special data pattern is transmitted which will allow the receiver circuits to determine the exact timing of the start of the first data byte in the block of data. Once this timing reference and the clock ra..e have been established the exact location of every other data byte in the block can be determined by counting bit periods, in groups of eight, starting from the timing reference point.

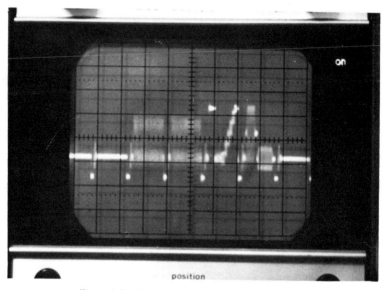

Figure 2.5   Teletext data waveform on oscilloscope

The synchronisation signals take up three bytes of data at the start of each data row. A further two bytes are used to provide a row address or identification code which tells the decoder system where that particular row of text must be displayed on the screen. Thus there are a total of 45 bytes, or 360 bits, of data in each teletext data line.

Teletext data signals

At the present time the data signals for teletext are inserted on lines 17/18 during even field scans and 330/331 on odd scans. It is possible that in the future more scan lines may be used for teletext data to allow an increase in the amount of information provided on a channel.

To cater for this the specification allows for teletext data to be inserted on any lines from 7 to 22 and 320 to 335 during the blanking intervals of a 625 line signal.

The data level for a logic 0 signal is at the black level of the television picture signal. A logic 1 data signal will be at approximately 66% of the peak white level of the picture signal. The data signals use the Non Return to Zero (NRZ) format where the signal level remains at either the 1 or 0 level through each bit period. If several bits at 1 follow one another the signal merely remains at the 1 level for the required number of bit periods.

In the 625 line system a single line scan has a period of 64 micro-seconds of which 52 microseconds are available for the insertion of data signals. With a total of forty-five data bytes for each row of text, and assuming that a row of text occupies one scan line, the data rate for a teletext signal is 6.9375 megabits per second. This gives a time period of some 144 nanoseconds for each data bit.

Pulse shape and bandwidth

Before transmission the logic signals consist of a sequence of square edged pulses as shown in *Figure 2.6a*. The highest frequencies will be produced when the data consists of a sequence of alternate 1 and 0 bits.

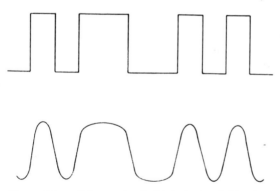

Figure 2.6   Teletext signals (a) logic signal (b) raised cosine data signal as transmitted

If such a signal is analysed it can be seen to be built up from a funda-mental sine wave having a frequency equal to half the bit rate and a series of harmonic components. For teletext the fundamental component is 3.46875 MHz and the harmonics may extend up to some 30 to 50 MHz. If such a signal were transmitted the higher frequency components would be lost due to the bandwidth limitations of both the transmitter and receiver systems.

If with an alternate 1 and 0 bit pattern signal only the fundamental at 3.46875 MHz were transmitted the resultant signal would be a sine wave where the positive half cycles represented 1 bits and negative half cycles correspond to 0 bits. It would still be possible to differentiate between 1 and 0 signals provided that the signal is sampled at roughly the centre of each bit period. The original logic signal could now be reconstructed from the received signal.

Actual teletext data signals are filtered in this way before transmission and the resultant pulses have a wave shape generally known as 'raised cosine'. The filter used has a frequency response as shown in *Figure 2.7*

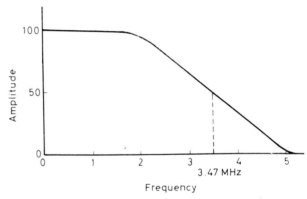

Figure 2.7   Frequency spectrum of a raised cosine data signal for teletext

and the data signals will be rounded off as shown in *Figure 2.6b*. These signals will readily pass through transmitter and receiver systems which have the proper bandpass characteristics for handling a 625 line television picture signal.

Eye height

In the analysis of the data signals it was assumed that the data consisted of a continuous stream of alternate 1 and 0 bits. In practice the signal is an irregular pattern of bits and a single 1 bit might produce a waveform roughly as shown in *Figure 2.8*. Here it is seen that there is an overshoot which will affect the following bit of the data pattern. In fact with an irregular data signal every pulse will influence the shape of all of the following pulses to some extent. The result is that the amplitude of the pulses and the mean level of the signal will vary according to the data patterns present. This effect is known as 'intersymbol interference'.

The effects of intersymbol interference can be examined by means of an 'eye height' display. Here the data signal is applied to the Y plates of an oscilloscope and the timebase for the X plates is set for two bit periods and synchronised to the incoming data. This effectively superimposes the wave shapes of successive pulses to produce a display as shown in *Figure 2.9*.

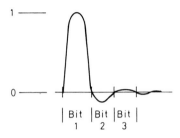

Figure 2.8   Shape of teletext pulses after filtering

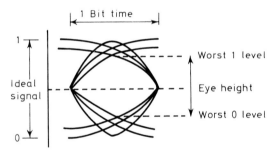

Figure 2.9   Eye height display showing the effect of intersymbol interference and receiver distortion

The central eye shaped area of the display in *Figure 2.9* shows the worst case levels of the 1 and 0 data pulses. With an ideal signal the clear central eye would extend up to the 1 signal level and down to the 0 level. Because of intersymbol interference the amplitude of data pulses does vary and the height of the clear eye is reduced. This 'eye height' gives a measure of signal distortion and as it is reduced the discrimination between 0 and 1 bits in the decoder system will become more difficult.

Band width limitations in the receiver i.f. amplifier will reduce the amplitude of short single bit pulses in the data stream and hence reduce the effective eye height. The phase characteristics of the amplifier are also important since a non linear phase response will cause some of the data transitions to be delayed thus making some of the data pulses narrower and making decoder timing critical. Non linear detector response will also reduce eye height although this problem is not frequently met in the newer receivers which have synchronous detectors for the video signal.

Eye height of a received signal is usually quoted as a percentage of the ideal signal amplitude. Normally the eye height will be around 60% to 80% in the service area but most receivers are likely to cope with eye heights as low as 25% without introducing noticeable display errors.

Parity bit

In teletext the eighth bit of each data byte is the parity bit which provides a facility for error detection. The state of this eighth bit is chosen so that the total number of bits at the 1 state in the byte is odd. If there are two 1 bits in the symbol code the parity bit would be set at 1 to produce three 1 bits in the complete byte. This scheme is known as an Odd Parity error detection system. It is equally possible to have an Even Parity error detection scheme where the total number of 1 bits in a byte is made even. Viewdata uses an even parity error check.

Errors occurring in the received data signal may be detected by using the parity bit. Firstly the total number of 1 bits in each data byte is checked. If the number is odd then the data is probably correct. If the parity test gives an even answer then the data is incorrect and will usually be rejected so that the incorrect signal is not displayed on the screen. This technique is effective in removing the occasional errors produced by interference pulses.

The parity bit may also perform another useful job in the teletext system. One of the disadvantages of using the NRZ method of data transmission is that if a stream of 1 bits follow one another the data level merely stays at 1 for a number of bit periods. To detect individual bits in the stream the receiver must sample the incoming signal during each bit period. If the clock timing is synchronised only at the start of the data line this imposes very tight accuracy requirements on clock timing and would make the design of the decoding clock circuit very difficult. When odd parity is used however there must be at least one and not more than seven 1 bits in each data byte. Thus a data transition must occur in each data byte and this may be used to resynchronise the clock to the data signal.

Chapter 3

Data Acquisition

In order to receive and display teletext information a specially adapted television receiver will be required. *Figure 3.1* shows a block system diagram of those parts of a teletext receiver which are involved in dealing with the teletext information.

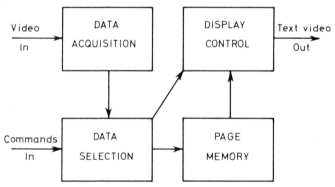

Figure 3.1   Block diagram of teletext decoder

Since the teletext data signals are transmitted as an integral part of the normal television signal the receiver section, consisting of tuner and i.f. amplifier, is basically the same as for a normal colour receiver. Some attention is needed here to ensure that the bandpass and group delay characteristics of the i.f. amplifier are correct but often if a good colour picture is produced then reception of the teletext data is also good.

The data signals are separated from the rest of the video signal in the data acquisition block. Here the text data signals are processed to convert them in to a stream of parallel data words and to generate the required timing signals to permit correct decoding of the received data.

Selection of the data for the particular page of text requested by the viewer is carried out in the next block labelled Data Selection. Once the required page of text data has been detected it is passed to the Page Memory where it is stored. A memory system is needed here because any given page is transmitted only once every thirty seconds or so whereas the display system needs continuous access to the data in order to produce a refreshed display once for every field scan of the picture tube.

The main function of the display block is to convert data signals from the page memory into a video signal which will produce the display of a page of text on the screen. When the receiver is operating in the text mode the picture video signal is disconnected from the video amplifier and is replaced by the text video signal from the display block. Since the display of text may be in colour the video signals for the text display will consist of red, green and blue components. Control signals from the display logic may also be used to switch the mode from picture to text during a display scan so that text can be inserted into the normal programme picture to present subtitle or newsflash information.

Data acquisition

The first stage in the processing of the teletext data is that of data acquisition. *Figure 3.2* shows in more detail the functions of a typical data acquisition system for a teletext decoder.

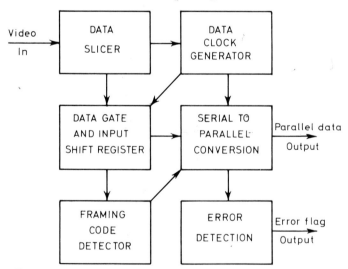

Figure 3.2   Block diagram of the data acquisition dection of a decoder

When received the teletext data is accompanied by the picture and sync. signals. In order that it can be dealt with by logic circuits is must first of all be converted to a sequence of '1' and '0' logic level signals. This is done by passing the combined signal through a 'data slicer'. The next stage is to remove those components produced by the picture signal. To achieve this the combined logic signal is passed through a gate which allows signals through only during those scan lines where teletext signals can be expected to appear.

Data slicer

When received from the video detector stage the text data signal will consist of a series of rather rounded off pulses sitting above the black level of the video signal. Often the complete video signal will have a d.c. offset of perhaps three or four volts relative to ground level giving a signal roughly as shown in *Figure 3.3*.

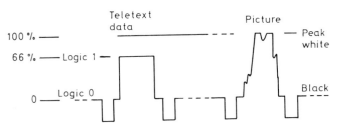

Figure 3.3   Teletext and picture video signals

On typical receivers the peak to peak amplitude of the video signal may be anything from about 1 to 3 volts. Since the data signal has an amplitude which is 50% of the total swing between peak white and the sync pulse tips it is likely that the peak to peak amplitude of the data pulses will be some 0.5 to 1.5 volts. This data signal must now be converted into a logic signal with a '0' level of about 0 volts and a '1' level of perhaps +5 volts.

Ideally the transitions between the '0' and '1' levels of the logic signal should be instantaneous so that the resultant logic signal is a square wave. At the same time the transitions should occur as nearly as possible at the same points as in the original logic signal inserted at the transmitter.

Suppose for the moment that the d.c. offset of the data can be removed so that the text signal swings equally about the 0 volt line. Now assuming that the signals have remained symmetrical about zero during the transmission and reception stages the points at which the received signal passes through the 0 volt level will be the same as the transition points of the original logic signal before transmission. All that has happened is that the signal has been rounded off on its peaks and troughs.

Suppose this data signal is fed to a simple transistor amplifier stage as shown in *Figure 3.4*. We shall assume that the transistor has a very

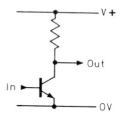

Figure 3.4   Simple data slicer

high gain and that it will start to conduct as soon as the input voltage to the base rises above the 0 volt level. As the data signal goes positive the transistor will turn on and its collector votlage will fall rapidly to the 0 volt level. When the data signal goes negative the transistor will cut off and the collector voltage will rise to the +5 volt supply level. Now as the data signal swings positive and negative the output collector voltage will be switched between 0 volts and +5 volts to produce a logic level signal.

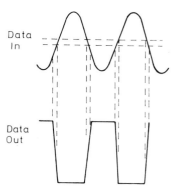

Figure 3.5   Waveforms for a simple slicer

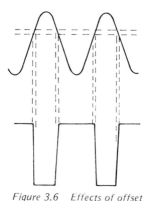

Figure 3.6   Effects of offset of the slicing level

In effect the transistor stage is amplifying a tiny slice through the data signal as shown in *Figure 3.5*. If the stage gain is high the slice will be very thin and the output will be virtually a square wave. It is because of this action that the circuit is generally referred to as a 'data slicer'.

Our simple transistor stage will in fact produce a '1' level at its output for a '0' data signal input but this can easily be corrected by adding a further transistor stage to invert the sense of the output signals.

In practice the input to the base of a typical silicon transistor will need to rise to about +0.1 volt before collector current will flow. This has the effect of moving the slice up into the positive half cycle of the data signal and the points at which the output level switches will no longer be at the correct times as is shown in *Figure 3.6.*

Emitter-coupled slicer

A rather more elegant and effective form of 'data slicer' circuit makes use of a pair of transistors with a common emitter coupling as shown in *Figure 3.7.*

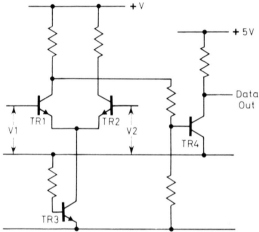

Figure 3.7   Typical emitter coupled comparator

The common emitter point is returned to a negative supply rail through transistor TR3 which forms a 'constant current' source. Since both TR1 and TR2 pass their emitter current through TR3 the latter will control the total current flowing in TR1 and TR2.

Suppose that the input voltages *V1* and *V2* applied to the bases of TR1 and TR2 are both set at 0 volts. In this type of circuit TR1 and TR2 would normally be chosen so that their gain and input characteristics were matched. Since the inputs are equal the two collector currents will also be equal and will each have a value equal to half of the current flowing through TR3. The collector voltages of TR1 and TR2 will also be equal and by proper choice of collector load resistors can be arranged to be at half the positive supply voltage.

If the input voltage *V1* is now made positive with respect to *V2* the current flowing in transistor TR1 will increase. Since the total current in TR3 is constant TR2 must now draw less current. As a result the collector voltage of TR1 will fall and that of TR2 will rise. As input *V1* is increased this action will continue until TR1 takes all of the current from TR3 whilst TR2 is completely cut off.

When input *V1* is driven negative relative to input *V2* the reverse action will occur. Now current through TR2 will increase and that through TR1 decreases until eventually TR2 takes all of the current from TR3 and TR1 is cut off.

This type of circuit is generally called a comparator since it effectively compares the input voltages *V1* and *V2*. If we use this circuit in place of the simple transistor slicer the problems due to *Vbe* offset disappear since as soon as *V1* changes relative to *V2* the output at the collectors of TR1 and TR2 will change.

Voltage *V2* can be considered as a reference level at which the circuit will operate. Using this type of slicer we can readily cope with the d.c. bias on the video signal from the detector stage by making *V2* equal to the bias level. Normally *V2* would be made variable so that it can be adjusted to place the slice level at the optimum point in the data signal.

To produce logic output signals at the proper levels the output from one of the collectors of the comparator is used to drive a single transistor stage as shown in *Figure 3.7*. In practical circuits there might be two or three emitter coupled stages in the comparator in order to obtain a high gain and hence produce a thin slice through the data signal.

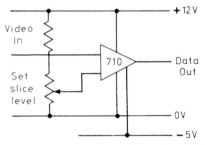

Figure 3.8   Practical data slicer using a 710

Comparator circuits using this principle are built as integrated circuits and typical of those available is the 710. This device has an effective gain of the order 1000 so that input signals of plus or minus a few millivolts at the input will cause the output to switch from one logic level to the other.

Figure 3.8 shows a practical data slicer circuit in which a 710 type comparator is used.

In most cases the input impedance presented by a comparator circuit tends to be rather low and it is usual to drive it from an emitter follower stage coupled to detector output. Direct coupling is normally used to avoid problems which can be produced by using R—C coupling. If R—C coupling is used the d.c. component of the signal is lost and the mean d.c. level of the data signal is likely to vary with the pattern of '1's and '0's in the data. As a result the slice level effectively moves up and down within the data signal which can produce timing problems and data errors unless some action is taken to restore the proper d.c. level conditions at the comparator side of the coupling capacitor.

Adaptive data slicers

In a typical receiver system the exact d.c. level of the video signal may change slightly with time due to temperature effects or to changes in the received signal level. Although the a.g.c. system can usually cope with a wide variation in signal level there will be some small change in mean level at the detector as the a.g.c. operates.

These small level changes may have little effect upon the displayed picture but changes of perhaps 50 to 100 mV in the d.c. level of the data signals may upset the slicing level and produce errors in the decoded data. Often this effect occurs on switching from one channel to another and with a simple slicer circuit this could mean that the slice level needs to be adjusted for each individual channel.

In order to cope with signal level variations at the video detector a rather more sophisticated form of slicer circuit may be used. Instead of using a fixed d.c. voltage as the reference level for the comparator the reference voltage is derived from the signal itself. This type of data slicer circuit is called an 'adaptive' slicer and a typical arrangement would be as shown in *Figure 3.9*.

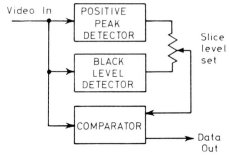

Figure 3.9   Block diagram for an adaptive data slicer

A peak detector is used to sense the peak amplitude of the data pulses and produces a proportional d.c. output voltage. A second detector is used to produce an output corresponding to the black level of the picture signal. These voltages are fed to a resistor chain from which a reference signal for the comparator is derived. Normally the reference level will be set roughly halfway between the black level voltage and the peak voltage to give the proper slice level.

With this circuit, if the mean d.c. level of the video signal changes the slice level reference will also change in sympathy so that the slicing level remains at the same point in the signal waveform. Similarly if the signal amplitude changes the reference level will also be altered to maintain the slice level at roughly half the peak amplitude of the data pulses.

Data gate

The logic signals produced by the data slicer will contain not only the text data but also the sliced version of the picture signal. Since this signal might confuse the decoding logic the picture component must be removed.

Teletext data signals can be expected to occur on any of the field blanking lines from line 7 (320) up to line 22 (335). The simplest arrangement for gating out the picture components uses a monostable delay circuit as shown in *Figure 3.10*. Here the monostable is triggered

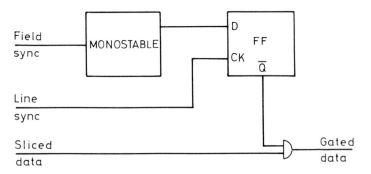

Figure 3.10   Monostable type data gate

by field sync pulses and is arranged to time out some time during line 22 (335) of the field scan. The output from this monostable feeds the D input of a flip-flop which is clocked by line sync pulses and the flip-flop in turn controls a gate in the data line feeding the decoder circuits.

After the field sync pulse the monostable is set and the D flip-flop will be clocked into the 1 state by each line sync pulse. Thus the data gate is opened and allows text data to pass through to the decoding logic. During line 22 (335) of the field scan the monostable resets and the D input of the flip-flop falls to 0. Now on the next line sync pulse, at the start of line 23 (336), the flip-flop will be reset and will close the data gate preventing the following components from reaching the decoding logic.

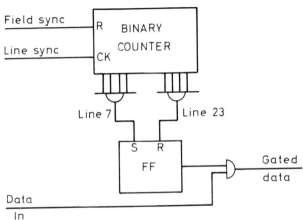

Figure 3.11   Counter type data gate

An alternative approach is shown in *Figure 3.11* in which the delay is produced by counting line sync pulses and using two flip-flops to control the data gate.

Clock synchronisation

Having produced from the data slicer a logic signal which represents the stream of text data the next step is to identify the logic state of each of the individual data bits in the line of text data.

With NRZ coding if a number of successive data bits in the line are '1's the logic level will merely stay at '1' for the appropriate number of bit periods. Similarly a string of '0's produces a continuous '0' level. Under these conditions there is no built in timing information which will enable individual bits to be identified.

To identify the bit states correctly we need to take a sample of the logic level during each bit period. This can be achieved by using a locally generated clock which produces pulses at the bit rate of

6.9375 MHz. For proper operation this clock must be synchronised to the incoming data. Ideally the sample pulse should occur at the middle of each bit period of the received signal.

At the start of every line of text data the first two words consist of alternate '1' and '0' bits as shown in *Figure 3.12*. These two words are known as the 'clock run in' and are used to synchronise the bit sampling clock in the decoder.

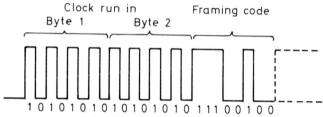

Figure 3.12   Clock run-in and framing code bytes

Since there is a data transition at the end of every bit period in these two words they can be used to determine the relative phase of the local clock oscillator and to lock it into correct synchronisation with the incoming data.

Once the synchronisation of the local clock circuit has been established at the start of the data line it can be maintained throughout the rest of the line by using the logic level transitions that occur in the text data as a timing reference. The teletext coding has been so arranged that at least one logic level transition will occur within each eight bit data byte.

Simple L–C clock generator

Perhaps the simplest form of clock generator makes use of an ordinary L–C tuned circuit which is tuned to 6.9 MHz and shock excited by pulses derived from the received data. *Figure 3.13* shows the general idea.

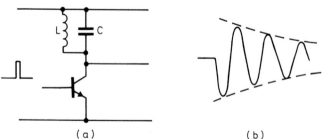

(a)   (b)

Figure 3.13   Simple L-C clock generator (a) circuit; (b) waveform

When a short pulse of energy is applied, through the transistor, to the tuned circuit an oscillation will be set up at the natural resonant frequency of the tuned circuit. This produces a sine wave voltage across the capacitor. If the circuit were perfect these oscillations, once started, would go on for ever. In practice energy is dissipated in the resistance of the coil and in the capacitor leakage so the amplitude of the oscillations slowly dies away to zero as shown in *Figure 3.13*.

The rate at which the amplitude of the oscillations decays is governed by the operating Q of the tuned circuit. Amplitudes of successive peaks can be determined roughly by the equation;

$$\frac{A_{n+1}}{A_n} = \epsilon^{\frac{-\pi}{Q}}$$

Where A_n is the amplitude of one peak and A_{n+1} that of the next peak.

Figure 3.14 shows a practical clock generator using this principle. Transistor TR1 acts as a phase splitter and is fed by data signals from the output of the slicer. The signal from the emitter of TR1 is differentiated

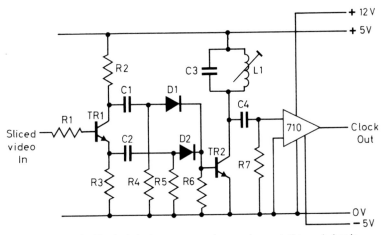

Figure 3.14   Typical clock generator scheme using an L-C tuned circuit

by C2, R5 to produce a short positive pulse each time the data signal switches from '0' to '1'. Inverted data pulses from the collector are differentiated by C1, R4 to produce short positive pulses on the data transitions from '1' to '0'. The diodes D1 and D2 pass these short positive pulses to the base of TR3 which then excites the tuned circuit L1, C3 to make it oscillate at the bit frequency of 6.9375 MHz.

The sine wave produced by the tuned circuit couples via C4 to one input of a 710 comparator. At this point the signal will swing symmetrically about 0 V so the reference input of the 710 is also set at 0 V. A slice will now be taken through the zero crossing points of the sine wave to produce a square wave clock signal at the 710 output.

Phase locked clock generators

An alternative approach to the generation of the bit clock is to use a phase locked voltage controlled oscillator as shown in *Figure 3.15*.

Here use is made of the fact that the bit frequency is exactly 444 times the line scan frequency. The output of the oscillator is divided in frequency by 444 time to give an output at line scan frequency. This

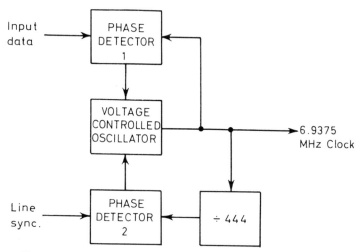

Figure 3.15   Clock generator using voltage-controlled oscillator (VCO)

signal is compared with the timing of the line sync pulses and a voltage is produced which is proportional to the frequency error. This voltage is fed back to the oscilllator to control the clock frequency until it is exactly 444 times line scan frequency. A second carrier detector compares the phase of the oscillator with the incoming data bits and produces a further error correction signal to lock the clock into synchronism with the data.

Another approach might be to use a crystal controlled oscillator in a similar arrangement to that used for the colour reference oscillator in the chrominance circuits. In this case the clock run in pattern is used in the same way as the colour burst to phase lock the oscillator.

Word synchronisation

Having synchronised the local decoding clock the next step is to locate and separate out from the data stream each of the eight bit data bytes that represent the text symbols.

In order to locate accurately the start of the first data word a specially coded byte of data, called the Framing Code byte, is included immediately after the clock run in pattern as shown in *Figure 3.12*. The pattern of bits in this Framing Code is 11100100.

At this point the decoder circuits must search through the incoming stream of data bits for the Framing code pattern. When the pattern is detected one particular bit in the data can be pinpointed as a timing reference from which the exact position of every following data byte in the row can be located.

Input shift register

In order to detect the Framing Code pattern we need to be able to freeze the incoming stream of data in some way so that it is possible to examine the states of eight successive bits in the data stream simultaneously. This is easily achieved by making use of a shift register.

A shift register consists basically of a number of D type flip-flops connected in cascade as shown in *Figure 3.16*. Each D input in driven from the Q output of the preceding stage and all flip-flops are clocked in parallel by the clock pulse.

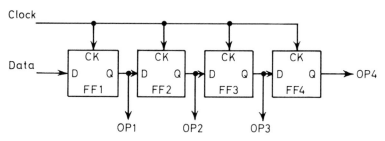

Figure 3.16   Four D-type flipflops connected to form a serial shift register

When a clock pulse is applied each flip-flop will take up the state of the preceding flip-flop in the chain. Thus the pattern of data states moves along the register by one stage each time a clock pulse is applied. This is shown in *Figure 3.17* where the states of the flip-flops in an eight stage shift register are shown for a number of clock cycles. The shift

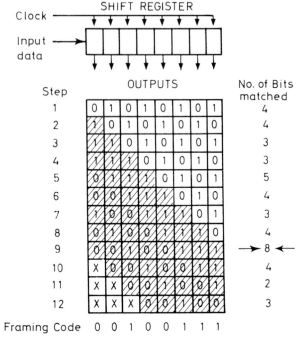

Figure 3.17   *Pattern of bits in the input shift register as the framing code passes through it*

register will now contain a bit pattern showing the state of the input signal at the time of each of the last eight clock pulses. In the case of a teletext signal where the clock is synchronised to the data the shift register will contain the pattern of the last eight bits of data received. Now it is possible to search for the Framing Code pattern.

Framing code detector

To detect the presence of the framing code pattern in the input shift register a simple coincidence gate circuit as shown in *Figure 3.18* can be used.

Here an 8 input NAND gate is used to detect a match with the Framing Code pattern. This gate will produce '0' output only when all of its inputs are at the '1' level.

Assuming that the Framing Code is already properly lined up in the input shift register the states of the individual flip-flops will be as shown. Where the bit of the Framing Code stored in the register should be a '0' the output of that flip-flop is inverted before it is fed to the input of the NAND gate. Now when the Framing Code pattern is correctly located in the shift register all of the inputs to the NAND gate will be at '1' and its output will fall to '0'.

Figure 3.17 shows the patterns of bits in the input shift register as the Framing Code passes through it. Only in one position will all eight bits of the pattern match, to give a '0' pulse out of the detector gate. In

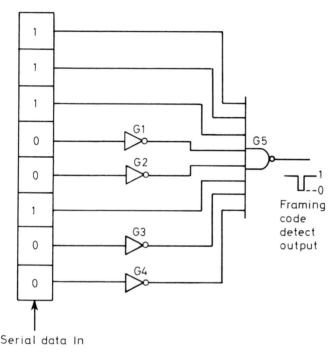

Serial data In

Figure 3.18   Framing code detector showing states of shift register stages when the framing code is detected

all other positions there will be at least two bits mismatched. The bits marked X may be either '1' or '0' according to the pattern of the data word which follows the Framing Code.

To avoid detection of spurious Framing Code patterns within the text data it is usual to inhibit the action of the Framing Code detector just after the time when the Framing Code is normally expected within the line of data. When a valid Framing Code is detected the output pulse from the Framing Code detector is used to set a flip-flop which will indicate that the data for the row of text may now be accepted.

Serial to parallel conversion

For the remainder of the decoding process it is more convenient to have the data in parallel form on an eight wire data bus. The input shift register does in fact have parallel data at its outputs but the pattern changes once every bit period as incoming data moves along the register (*Figure 3.19*). The data for any given byte is therefore stable for only one bit period which gives insufficient time to process it.

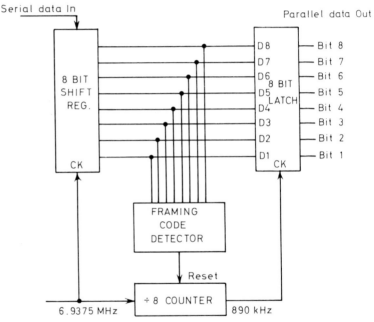

Figure 3.19   Serial to parallel conversion

At the point when the Framing Code is detected the data pattern for the Framing Code is static in the input shift register. Eight clock pulses later the first data byte of the row of text data will be static in this register and this could be transferred in parallel to another eight bit data register which will drive the data bus. Transfers of data to this output register can now be made at eight clock pulse intervals as each new byte becomes correctly lined up in the input shift register.

The clock pulses for the data transfer operation are produced by feeding the data clock to a divide by eight counter which produces one output pulse at every eighth input clock pulse. This counter is held reset from the line sync pulse until the Framing Code is detected so that the transfer pulse is properly synchronised to the incoming data. Data at the output is now static for eight clock periods which gives ample time to decode and store the data.

Error detection

In the final part of the data acquisition section the state of the parity bit is compared with the pattern of bits in the data byte to check for possible errors in reception.

Parity checking is carried out by using an array of Exclusive OR type gates. This type of gate produces a 1 at its output when only one of its two inputs is at the 1 level. If both inputs are at 1 or both are at 0 the gate output will be 0.

The basic arrangement for a four input parity check circuit is shown in *Figure 3.20*. The input data is divided up into pairs of bits and each

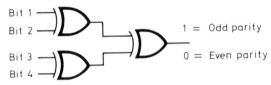

Figure 3.20   Basic 4 input parity detector

pair is fed to the inputs of an Exclusive OR gate. Each gate effectively carries out an odd parity check on its two input bits. For odd parity the gate output is 1 and for even parity it is 0. Now if the outputs of the pair of Exclusive OR gates are fed to a further Exclusive OR gate an odd parity check is carried out on the results of the first two checks. This gives the same result as carrying out an odd parity check on all four inputs simultaneously.

For an eight bit parity check the system is extended so that the outputs of the pair of four input parity checks are themselves fed to an Exclusive OR gate. This tree type of structure can be used to construct parity check systems for any number of bits.

When the output of the parity check circuit is at 1 this indicates that the data has odd parity and therefore may be accepted. This parity check signal is used to control the writing of text data into the page memory so that if an even parity condition is detected the data byte is not written into the memory and hence the erroneous symbol is not displayed on the screen.

For an even parity system such as that used in the Viewdata transmissions the same basic parity detection circuit is used but now a 0 at the output will indicate correct data and a 1 will indicate an error.

Chapter 4

Selecting the Page

Once teletext data bytes are available in sequence on the eight bit parallel data bus the next stage in the decoding process is to select out, from the stream of data bytes, those that correspond to the particular page of text requested by the viewer. Apart from selecting the required page the decoder must also be able to identify individual rows of text so that they can be displayed at their proper position on the screen.

To facilitate this selection process additional bytes of information

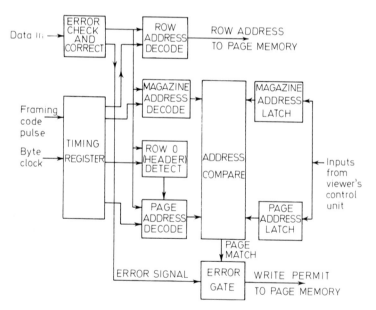

Figure 4.1   Block diagram of page selection system

are included to identify the page currently being transmitted and the individual row of text contained within the line of data.

Figure 4.1 shows the block diagram of those stages of a decoder concerned in selecting the page of data.

Row addressing

Within each page there are 24 rows of text and each row of 40 characters is transmitted as one scan line full of data. Each row is labelled with a unique address code which will enable the decoder to determine where the row of text must be displayed within the page.

Two data bytes immediately following the Framing Code pattern are used to carry the Row Address code. In order to identify the 24 rows they are labelled from 0 to 23 using a simple binary code. Five bits are used for this code which in fact allows for row addresses up to 31.

Error protection

At this point the effects of errors in the received data need to be considered. In the case of an error in a byte representing a text symbol the result will be that an incorrect symbol will be displayed in that position on the screen. If there are a few errors in a page of text this will result in some of the characters displayed wrongly but this may not be serious. The human brain is amazingly adept at anticipating what an incorrect letter should be merely from the pattern of the word containing it or from the context of the message being displayed. It is likely that the viewer may not even notice an occasional symbol error in the displayed page.

In the case of errors which occur in the data for a row or page address code however the results produced can be totally disastrous. When a row address is incorrectly received the row will probably be displayed in the wrong place on the screen and a few such errors can reduce the page of text to an almost meaningless jumble of words.

When a page address code is affected by errors the result is likely to be that the wrong page will be chosen for the display. This may result in random pages of text appearing on the screen from time to time instead of the requested one.

Although the parity error check, normally used on all data words could be used to suppress acceptance of rows or pages if the addresses were in error it is desirable that some better form of error protection be used on these codes.

Hamming codes

One possible solution to the problem of errors in the address codes would be to transmit each address code byte twice during each line of data. The two received codes are then compared in the decoder and if they match the address code is accepted as correct. This method of protection is not, however, as good as it might at first seem and after trials in the early versions of teletext it was rejected.

There is already in each data byte a parity check bit which allows single errors to be detected. If some further parity check bits are included in the byte it becomes quite possible not only to detect the error but to provide some degree of error correction as well. These error correcting codes are called Hamming codes after R. W. Hamming of Bell Telephone Laboratories who developed them for use in data transmission via the telephone system.

In Hamming coded address bytes only four of the bits are used to convey the message information whilst the other four bits provide error checking and correction. With these codes four separate parity checks are carried out upon the data within the byte (*Figure 4.2*).

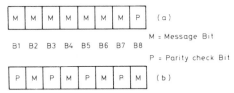

*Figure 4.2   Teletext data bytes (a) normal text
data; (b) Hamming coded address data*

One parity check is carried out over all eight bits of the byte in the same way as for normal text bytes. The other three checks are carried out on three groups of four bits within the byte. By examining the results of these four error checks it is possible, for a single bit error, to determine which bit is wrong and, by inverting the incorrect bit, to produce the correct data byte.

Figure 4.2 shows the structure of a Hamming coded address byte as used in the teletext system. The message and error check bits are interleaved so that bits 2, 4, 6 and 8 carry the address information whilst bits 1, 3, 5 and 7 are the results of four separate parity checks on the data byte.

Error correction

Each of the four error checks is made for an odd parity result. Bit 1 is the parity bit for check A which is carried out using bits 1, 2, 6 and 8 of the byte. Check B is carried out over bits 2, 3, 4 and 8 to produce a parity bit at position 2 in the byte. The third check (C) uses bits 2, 4, 5 and 6 to produce a result at the bit 5 position in the byte. Finally check D is carried out over all eight bits to produce bit 7 of the byte. These four error checks are summarised in *Figure 4.3*.

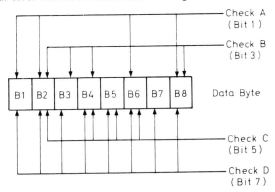

Figure 4.3   Hamming code parity checks

A	B	C	D	ACTION REQUIRED
0	0	0	0	DATA IS CORRECT
1	0	0	0	
0	1	0	0	
1	1	0	0	REJECT DATA
0	0	1	0	TWO OR MORE
1	0	1	0	ERRORS DETECTED
0	1	1	0	IN BYTE
1	1	1	0	
0	0	0	1	INVERT BIT 7
1	0	0	1	INVERT BIT 1
0	1	0	1	INVERT BIT 3
1	1	0	1	INVERT BIT 8
0	0	1	1	INVERT BIT 5
1	0	1	1	INVERT BIT 6
0	1	1	1	INVERT BIT 4
1	1	1	1	INVERT BIT 2

0 = Parity test O.K.

1 = Error detected

Figure 4.4   Results of parity tests and corrective action required

When these four error checks are carried out on the received data there are sixteen possible results which can occur and these are shown in *Figure 4.4*. Here a 0 is used to show that the parity check was correct whilst a 1 shows that the parity check failed indicating a data error.

Obviously when all four error checks are successful there is no error in the received data and the address can be accepted as being correct.

When check D fails this indicates that there is an error within the data byte. Examination of the results of the other three checks will allow the decoder to determine which bit is incorrect. Now if the state of this bit is inverted the data in the byte will be corrected.

To discover, in the case of a single bit error, which of the bits is wrong the decoder system simply checks to find which bit is common to all of the parity checks that show an error condition. *Figure 4.4*

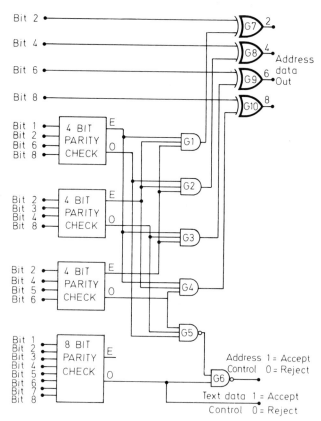

Figure 4.5   Logic scheme for error detection and correction of Hamming coded data

shows each of these possible combinations and indicates the particular bit that must be inverted to correct the error.

When check D is successful but one, or more, of the other parity checks fails an interesting situation arises. In this case there must be at least two errors in the data byte received. Check D, which tests all eight bits, is still successful because the two errors cancel one another and the total number of bits at '1' remains odd. When this occurs it is not possible to correct the errors so the byte of data must be rejected. A similar situation arises if there are four or six bits of the byte in error.

A typical system for detecting and correcting errors in the Hamming coded bytes is shown in *Figure 4.5*. Here the four bits corresponding to the message are fed via a set of Exclusive OR gates which act as switched inverters. In this type of gate if one input is held at '1' the signal at the other input will be inverted by the gate. The error outputs from the four parity check circuits are combined together in four AND gates to select which bit is to be inverted. In this case only the message bits are corrected since the error check bits have no further function in the decoding process. Gate 5 checks for possible double errors to control the acceptance or rejection of the Hamming coded data.

Detection of the row address

Each Hamming coded address byte produces four bits of address data. Because 5 bits are needed for the Row Address code this is transmitted as two Hamming coded bytes which follow the Framing code pattern. The bits in these two bytes are allocated as shown in *Figure 4.6*. The

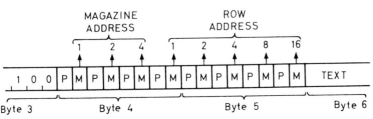

Figure 4.6   Allocation of bits in the magazine and row address bytes

three bits in the first word which are not used for row addressing are allocated as a Magazine identifier and are used as part of the page identification code. Both Row Address and Magazine code are transmitted with the least significant bit first.

To detect the row address data the two bytes which follow the Framing Code must be selected out and stored in a parallel data register. This can readily be done by using a shift register to provide appropriate timing pulses as shown in *Figure 4.7*.

When the Framing Code is detected the shift register is loaded with a '1' in its first stage and '0's in all its other stages. The shift register is clocked by the same pulse that transfers data on to the parallel data bus. Each time a new word is transferred the '1' in the shift register

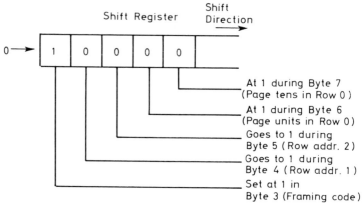

Figure 4.7   Principle of timing register

moves along by one stage. When the first row address data becomes available the '1' state will move to stage 2 of the shift register and this can be used to control the transfer of the four bits of address data into a separate address register. As the next data byte moves on to the data bus the shift register outputs a '1' at its third stage and transfers the second part of the row address data into the address register. The magazine and row address data will now be stored for the rest of the data line.

At this point the five bit row address code may be fed to the page memory circuits and will determine where the row of text is to be stored in the memory and hence where it will be displayed on the screen. This assumes, of course, that the page is the one requested by the viewer. The magazine code is passed to the page selection system where it is used as part of the page identification.

If an uncorrectable error is detected in either of these two address codes a flip-flop is set at '1' to act as an 'error flag'. When this error flag is at '1' the transfer of data to the memory or the selection of the page may be suppressed so that erroneous information is not stored in the page memory. The error flag is reset to '0' at the start of each new data line.

The header row

In the early version of Ceefax the page identification code was transmitted at the beginning of every text row in the same way as the row address code. Unfortunately this reduced the number of text characters that could be fitted into the row. In Oracle, on the other hand, the page code was transmitted only during the first row of text for the page and it was assumed that the following rows of text belonged to that same page. This technique has been used in the common teletext standard.

The top row of each teletext page is called the Header Row and has the address code 00000. Unlike the other rows it contains only 32 text characters instead of the normal 40. The first eight character positions in this row are used to carry a page number code, a time code and various control signals. Each of these first eight bytes are Hamming coded in the same way as the row and magazine address bytes.

Apart from the page number display the text in the header row is the same for every page. The normal layout consists of the name of the service (Ceefax or Oracle) followed by the page number, day and date and finally the time in hours minutes and seconds.

Page address

Figure 4.8 shows the layout of the additional address codes at the start of the header row. Immediately following the row address bytes

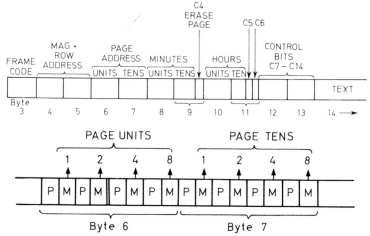

Figure 4.8   (a) Address codes in the header row; (b) Page address bit allocations

come two bytes which contain the page number of the page of text that is about to be transmitted.

Unlike the row address which is a five bit pure binary number the page code is transmitted in a format called Binary Coded Decimal or BCD. The average viewer needs to be able to select his desired page in decimal terms since very few people are conversant with binary numbers. Thus the user selects a page by keying in a series of decimal digits. Each decimal digit is converted into a 4 bit code in binary and the resultant groups of 4 bit binary numbers representing the original decimal digits are said to be in Binary Coded decimal format.

The page address codes consist of two Hamming coded bytes representing the units and tens of the decimal page number. Like the row address they are transmitted with the least significant bit first and with the units code first.

Following the page address are four bytes which give a time code in hours and minutes arranged as a four digit BCD code. Since there are only 60 minutes in the hour and the hours code is limited to 24 the number of bits needed for the tens digits of these codes is less than four. The unused bits in the Tens of Minutes and Tens of Hours bytes are used to provide control functions. The time code may be used as an extension of the page address to allow the selection of a much larger number of pages or it may be used as a real time code so that the page will be selected and displayed at some particular time chosen by the viewer or by the editor of the teletext service.

The two remaining bytes in the header row before the start of the text are used for control purposes to provide a number of special functions in the decoder if required.

Page selection

The process of selecting a particular page from the teletext service starts with the viewer who selects, using a calculator style keyboard, the digits of the page number that he wishes to view.

Each page in a transmitted teletext service can be identified by a combination of its page code digits in the header row and the magazine code transmitted at the start of every text row.

Since the magazine code consists of three binary bits it can have any value from 0 up to 7. This code is used as the hundreds digit of the page number. Thus page 123 will be identified as page code 23 and the magazine number 1.

Normally the magazine having the address code 000 is referred to as magazine 8 and the corresponding display of page numbers in the header row text will be in the range 800 to 899. When the viewer keys an eight for the hundreds digit of the page code the keyboard will produce the binary code 1000. Since the magazine address uses only the three least significant bits of this code however the decoder will search for the magazine address code 000. When this system of numbering is used all page numbers consist of three decimal digits which simplifies the coding circuits from the keyboard page selection system.

Magazine address data is selected out of the received data stream at the same time as the row address codes and is updated as each row of text is received. The page codes are selected out of the header row in much the same way and stored as two four bit binary numbers and this action is arranged to occur only when the row address code is 00000 corresponding to the header row.

When the viewer selects a new page the four bit binary patterns for each digit are stored in a series of four bit registers. During reception of the header row these codes are compared with the received magazine and page address codes. When a complete match occurs the data that follows is accepted and written into the page memory. When another header row is detected the codes are again compared and if a mismatch occurs the following data is ignored. Thus only the requested page of text is transferred to the memory and displayed. If an uncorrectable error occurs in any of the received address codes at this time the data will be ignored until the requested page header is repeated.

A typical logic circuit for detecting a match between two four bit binary patterns might use Exclusive OR gates as shown in *Figure 4.9*.

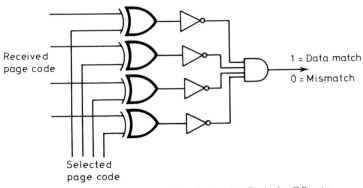

Figure 4.9   *Basic code comparison logic using Exclusive OR gates*

When the two inputs of this type of gate are at the same logic level, both at '1' or both at '0', the resultant gate output is '0'. Four of these gates can be used to compare a pattern of four bits in the received address code with the corresponding four bits in the page number selected by the viewer. When all four bits match the outputs from the four Exclusive OR gates will go to '0'. When inverted these will produce '1's at the four inputs of the AND gate and it will produce a '1' at its output to indicate a pattern match. Under all other input states the output of the AND gate will be at '0'.

If eleven Exclusive OR gates were used the patterns of the magazine and page codes in the header row could be compared with those of the requested page number. When a match occurs a '1' output will be produced and this could be used to set a flip-flop to indicate a 'page match' state. The flip-flop in turn could permit text data to be fed to the page memory until a new header row is detected. Thus the page of text selected by the viewer would be written into the page memory and displayed on the screen.

In practice it is usual to carry out the pattern match on the magazine codes separately and to combine the results with the page number match at the start of each text row. The general arrangement of the system is shown in *Figure 4.10*. Here the page codes are checked during

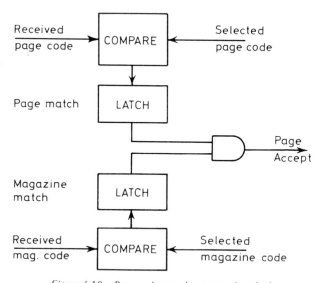

Figure 4.10   Page and magazine comparison logic

the header row and if a match occurs the 'page match' flip-flop is set to '1'. As each text row is received the magazine code is checked for a match and if this also checks with the requested code a 'row accept' flip-flop is set and text data for the row is transferred into the page memory.

Various other logic arrangements may be used for the pattern comparison. In some cases the data patterns may be compared sequentially as they appear on the eight bit wide parallel data bus. In each case the end result is the same.

Rolling header display

When a new page is selected by the viewer it is usual for the page memory to be cleared leaving a blank screen ready for the new page of text to be written when it is received. This can however have some disadvantages.

Normally the screen will remain blank until the new page is detected but this could take some 25 to 30 seconds with the average size magazine. If the selected page is not currently being transmitted then the screen will stay blank indefinitely which is rather annoying for the user.

To overcome this problem it is normal practice to arrange that when a new page is selected all header rows are displayed until the new page is found. The effect of this, as far as the viewer is concerned, is that the top row of display appears immediately although the rest of the screen remains blank. Since the format of all of the header rows is the same the only parts of the row that change will be the page number and the time display at the end of the row. When the selected page is received the page number will freeze and the rest of the page will appear. The time display will continue to update once a second to give a real time clock readout.

On early decoder systems the selection of pages was carried out by using a bank of thumbwheel switches. These switches would usually have a number display showing the page number selected. When a keyboard selection system is used however there is no indication of which keys have been pressed. Decoders using this form of data entry will usually be arranged to display the selected page number at the start of the header row using some of the symbol positions that have been allocated for the transmission of the address codes.

Row adaptive operation

For a 100 page magazine transmitted at a rate of four pages a second it will take 25 seconds to cycle through the set of pages. If more pages are included the waiting time before a newly selected page appears will be increased. In many pages however there may be several totally blank rows. If a text row is completely blank there is little point in transmitting it. The teletext specification therefore allows for blank lines within a page to be omitted from the data stream. Sometimes this can save some 20 to 25% of the time taken to transmit a magazine thus allowing more pages to be included without increasing the access time to a particular page.

This imposes some restrictions on the design of the decoder since it must be capable of dealing with a broken sequence of row addresses and the screen must be clear for a new page otherwise parts of the previously displayed page may be retained in the display.

Rotating pages

Often there may be several pages of text dealing with some common topic included within a teletext magazine. Of course these could be transmitted in the normal way using a series of separate page numbers and the viewer would then select the pages in turn to view them.

To save the viewer the need to continually change page numbers an alternative scheme is used. Here the pages are sent out in sequence using the same page number for the whole set. Each new page in the set is transmitted after a delay of perhaps a minute to allow the viewer to read the currently displayed page. The whole sequence of pages would then be repeated continuously.

As far as the viewer is concerned he would select the common page number and the series of pages with that number would automatically appear at intervals on his screen without any need to change the number of the page.

These multipage sets are generally referred to as 'rotating' or 'self-changing' pages. Usually there will be from two to six pages in the sequence but, in theory, there is no limit to the number of pages that may be included in a multipage set. In any magazine there may be several of these multipage sets interleaved with single pages of text. This allows the total number of different pages of text in a magazine to be increased without increasing the waiting time for access to any particular page number.

When a multiple set is selected by the viewer the page displayed will be the next one to appear in the sequence at the time he selects the page number.

Erase control bit

When a set of rotating pages is being transmitted and the row adaptive method of working is used problems can be encountered. If the screen is not cleared before each new page of text is written into the memory then where there are blank rows in the new page the previously stored text from the last page in the set will not be overwritten and will remain on the screen. Some means of telling the decoder to erase the display from the memory is required.

In the tens of minutes address code in the header row only three of the four bits are needed to handle the tens of minutes code. The fourth message bit in this address byte is used as an erase control code. When this bit is at '1' the decoder must erase its page memory for a new page of text to be written in.

When the erase bit is set at '1' the transmission sequence is adjusted so that a complete field scan period occurs before the new data for the page is transmitted. This allows the decoder one field scan in which to clear the page memory. Erasure of the memory is achieved by setting the memory into the writing mode and setting its data input to the code for a blank space. As the display screen scans the memory to produce the display the contents will be replaced by a page full of blank spaces.

When the row adaptive transmission mode is used it is normal to transmit the complete page, including blank rows, from time to time in order to clear up any errors that may have crept into the receiver display.

Chapter 5

The Page Memory

Television, like a cinema film, achieves the illusion of motion by representing a series of images on to the screen in rapid succession. Persistance of vision in the human eye merges these images together to produce what appears to be a moving picture. If the rate at which the pictures appear on the screen is too low the movements tend to become jerky and an objectionable flicker is produced. To overcome this television produces pictures at the rate of fifty a second, each picture being scanned in a series of horizontal lines.

When a television programme is transmitted, the video signal for a complete scan of the picture is sent out once every fiftieth of a second and at the receiver this signal is used to directly control the brightness of the display as the scanning beam passes over it.

In teletext the page of text symbols is produced in the same way as a television picture by modulating the brightness of the display as it is scanned. During each scan the data representing the text symbols on the page must also be scanned fifty times a second in sympathy with the display scan. This is where we meet a timing problem. The data for any selected page of text is transmitted only once every minute or so. In order to supply a continuous series of data for the display system some sort of memory is needed which can capture the data for a complete page of text and store it. Data from the memory can then be used to drive the display system every fiftieth of a second.

Memory requirements

Having decided that a memory system is needed for the production of a continuous text display the next step is to consider the size of the memory.

A page of teletext information has a rigidly defined format in which there are 24 rows of text with 40 symbols in each row. Each of these symbols is defined by a seven bit binary data code. Of course many of the symbol spaces in the page may be blank but a binary code is still needed to tell the display system to leave that space on the page display blank.

For a complete page therefore there will be 960 data codes required to define all of the displayed information. Since each code has seven data bits the page memory system must be capable of storing 960 × 7 or a total of 6720 bits of digital data.

Usually the decoder will have a memory which will hold just one page of text data but some decoder units may have much larger memories capable of storing four or even eight different pages of text. The principles involved in these larger memories are however exactly the same as for a single page memory.

Basically the memory unit will consist of an array of 960 electronic 'pigeonholes' each of which will be used to hold the data for one of the symbols on the page. Each of these memory slots will correspond to one particular symbol space in the display. Now as the data for each symbol of the selected page of data is received it will be placed in the appropriate memory slot. Similarly as each symbol space is scanned on the display the appropriate symbol code is read out from the memory to define which symbol is to be displayed in that space. To achieve this some means of addressing each individual location in the memory array is required.

Dynamic memory cell

One of the earliest ways in which electricity was stored was in a Leyden jar. Basically this is a capacitor, so maybe we could use a capacitor as a memory cell. *Figure 5.1* shows how a simple capacitor memory cell

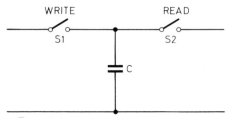

Figure 5.1   A simple capacitor memory cell

could be produced. For storing binary data only two states of the cell are required. When the capacitor is charged the cell can be considered to have a '1' bit stored in it whilst if the capacitor is discharged the stored bit of data will be considered to be a '0'.

To write a data bit into the memory cell the Write switch S1 is closed and the capacitor is connected to the data input signal and will charge or discharge until it reaches the same data state as the input. Now if the switch S1 is opened the capacitor will retain its state since there is no path through which it can charge or discharge. To read data from the memory cell the 'Read' switch S2 is closed and the capacitor is connected to the output line.

Unfortunately a large array of capacitors and switches is not a very practical proposition for use as a teletext page memory since there would need to be more than 6000 such cells. The switches could easily be replaced by field effect transistors, of which many thousands can readily be fabricated on a tiny slice of silicon. Low value capacitors can also be built into a silicon chip. Thus it is possible to build a large array of memory cells on a silicon chip to produce an integrated circuit memory device.

Figure 5.2 shows a typical circuit arrangement for a single memory cell using FETs and a capacitor to form the memory element. A typical

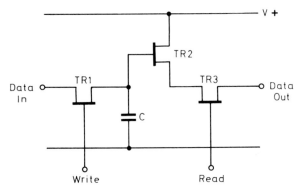

Figure 5.2   FET/Capacitor memory cell

integrated circuit memory which uses this type of cell is the Intel 1103. This contains an array of 1024 memory cells plus some addressing and control circuits and is packed on to a slice of silicon only 3 mm ($\frac{1}{8}$ in) square. *Figure 5.3* shows the layout of the circuits on the chip. The regular pattern produced by the memory cells can easily be seen.

Consider now the action of the memory cell shown in *Figure 5.2*. If a voltage is applied to the 'Write Select' input line then transistor TR1 will be turned on and will effectively connect the capacitor to the input data line. The capacitor will now charge or discharge until it has the same state as the input data. When the 'Write Select' input is removed the capacitor is disconnected from the input data line and stores the logic state that has been written into it. Transistor TR2 acts as a source follower. It will present a high impedance to the capacitor to prevent the stored charge leaking away and at the same time is able to a low impedance voltage output corresponding to the charge on the capacitor. Transistor TR3 acts as a series switch in the output line and

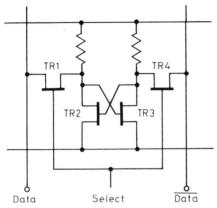

Figure 5.3   Static memory cell

is primarily used to select the cell for reading when a number of similar cells are connected in parallel to a common output data line. By applying a signal to the 'Read Select' line the transistor TR3 is turned on and the state of the stored charge on the capacitor can be read out to the output data line without affecting the state of the capacitor itself.

Selecting the cell

When a large array of cells is used to form a memory it is usual to bring together the input lines for all of the cells to produce a single input data line. Similarly the outputs from the cells would also be joined in parallel. Now a method is needed to select which cell is to be read from or written into. We could of course bring out all of the individual 'Read Select' and 'Write Select' control lines but for an array of say 1000 cells this would require some 2000 lead-out wires from the integrated circuit which is not very practical.

Usually the memory cells are connected in an array of rows and columns as shown in *Figure 5.4*. Here there are sixteen cells connected in a four by four array. The individual cells are selected by using a row and column addressing scheme. Suppose we want to write data into the cell marked 6. Firstly the input 'Row Select' switch for Row 2 would be made to connect the input data to the cells in Row 2.

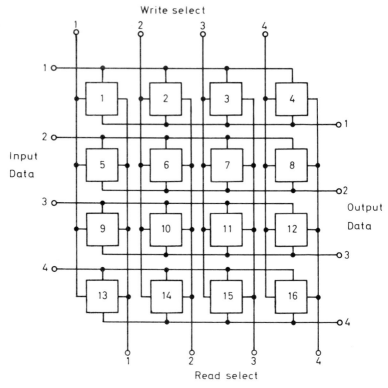

Figure 5.4   Row and column addressing

Next the 'Write Select' lines for all of the cells in Column 2 would be energised and as a result the input data will be written into cell number 6. The 'Write Select' input will not affect the charge on any of the other cells in column 2 because their input data line is not connected.

Selecting a cell for reading is carried out in much the same way by activating the appropriate 'Read Select' and 'Output Row Select' switches. The 'Input' and 'Output Row Select' lines could in fact be common and it is also possible to use common select lines for column selection in the 'Read' and 'Write' modes. Now only eight cell addressing lines are needed instead of sixteen or thirty two. This saving will be greater for the larger arrays so that an array of 1024 cells would need only 32 + 32 or 64 address lines.

Even with 64 address lines the integrated circuit is still rather unwieldy. The number of address wires can be reduced still further by using a binary coding scheme to decide which of the row or column select switches is to be turned on. For our 16 cell array a two bit binary number is sufficient to identify all of the row select lines and a second two bit number could be used for column select. This reduces the number of address wires to four and in the case of 1024 cell array the number of address inputs is reduced to only ten lines. Now it becomes possible to build the 1024 cell memory device into a standard 16 pin dual in line integrated circuit package.

Since each array of cells stores only one bit of the symbol data we shall need seven 1024 cell memory arrays to cope with the data for a page of text. The seven separate memory units would now be addressed in parallel so that a single bit is taken from the same cell position in each of the seven memories and the seven data bits are then output on seven separate data lines. Thus our complete page store system has been reduced to just seven 16 pin integrated circuits.

Static memories

One problem with memory cells which use a capacitor as the storage element is that the capacitor will slowly lose its charge due to leakage currents in the circuit. In fact, because the capacitors in an integrated circuit memory are relatively low in value, the data may become unreliable after only a few milliseconds of storage time.

To overcome this difficulty it is usually arranged that data in this type of memory is regularly read from the cells and then written back into them thus topping up the charge on the capacitor. This 'refreshing' action is usually carried out automatically each time the cells are accessed for reading. In order to save time a whole row or column of cells will be refreshed simultaneously but this action will need to be repeated every few milliseconds. This continual refreshing of the data gives this type of memory cell the name dynamic.

An alternative way of producing a memory cell is to build a flip-flop circuit into each cell; the circuit will be as shown in *Figure 5.3*. The flip-flop consisting of transistors TR2 and TR3 has two stable states where one of the transistors is turned on and the other is turned off. To write data into the cell the input signal is connected to the two data lines which are connected in parallel to every cell in the memory array. A cell select signal derived from the memory addressing system turns on TR1 and TR4 so that the flip-flop transistors TR2 and TR3 are forced to take up the state of the input data.

When the input data is disconnected, or another cell addressed, the flip-flop will store the data that has been written into it for an indefinite period. To read data from the cell the data lines are connected to the memory output terminals and the cell is again selected. Now the state of the flip-flop can be read out without altering the stored data.

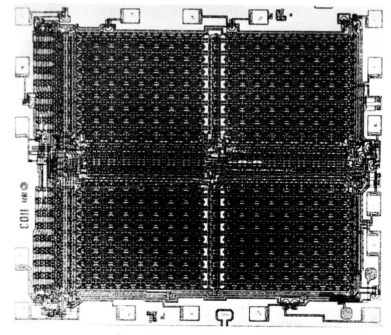

Figure 5.5   Intel 1103 memory chip

Static memory arrays are addressed in much the same way as the dynamic types by using a row and column select system.

Typical of this type of memory is the 2102 which has 1024 memory cells and comes in a sixteen pin DIL package as shown in *Figure 5.6*. It is also possible to obtain a memory with 4096 cells. The 2114 has four separate 1024 cell memory arrays in the same device so that it can accept four bit binary data words. In order to cope with the extra inputs

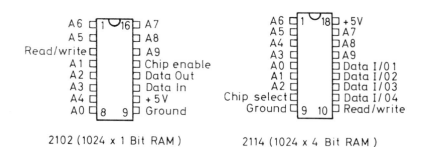

Figure 5.6   Typical memory devices

and outputs this device uses an 18 pin package and the input/output data lines share common terminal pins as can be seen from the connection diagram of *Figure 5.6.*

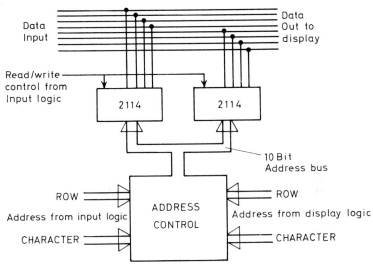

Figure 5.7   Typical page memory system

When data is to be written into the 2114 its output circuits are disabled so that they do not affect the input data lines. Using the 2114 only two memory chips will be needed for a complete page memory for teletext. A typical arrangement might be as shown in *Figure 5.7.*

Address generation

Integrated circuit memory devices were originally developed for use in computer systems and are arranged to have a square array of memory cells and a binary number of cells in the array.

A typical memory device, capable of holding a page of teletext data, might have 1024 cells arranged in 32 columns and 32 rows. Unfortunately the data for our teletext page is arranged as 24 rows and 40 columns which is not entirely compatible with the memory address system. In order to fit the data into the page memory the character and row numbers of the teletext address system will need to be modified in some way to match them to the 32 × 32 memory address. It is a pity that the memory could not be organised as 40 columns and 24 rows but at present such devices are not available.

There are two basic ways in which the teletext row and character addresses can be modified to produce the new address needed for the page memory. In the first method the symbol codes are written into consecutive addresses in the page memory from 000 up to 959.

For the first text row the character count is simply used as the memory address. On the second text row forty must be added to the character count to produce the correct memory address and for each

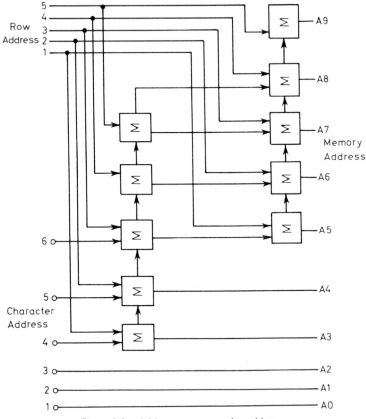

Figure 5.8   Address generator using adders

succeeding row another forty is added to the memory address. This can be achieved by using a pair of binary address adders as shown in *Figure 5.8*. Here the row address is added to the character count in the first adder. However the row address lines are offset by three bits relative to the character count so that the 1 bit of the row address is added to the 8 bit of the character count. This produces the effect that when the row address increases by 1 it will cause 8 to be added to the character address. We have effectively added eight times the row address to the character address.

A similar action takes place in the second adder but this time the row address is added in at the 32 level of the second adder's input. This produces the effect of adding a further 32 times the row address to the output of the first adder. At the final output an address is produced which is 40 (32 + 8) times the row address plus the character count and each symbol will now be written into a consecutive location in the range 000 to 959 as required.

An alternative approach is to use the character count and row address of the teletext page to provide the column and row addresses of the page memory directly. Now the first 32 characters in each text row will

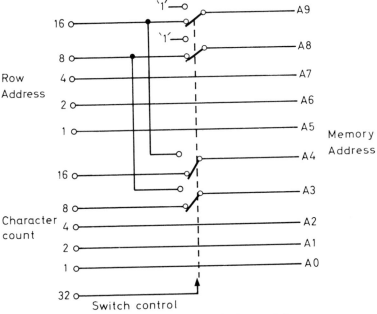

Figure 5.9   Address control using a switch

be written into each of the first 24 rows of the page memory. This leaves 8 rows of the page memory unused. The remaining eight characters for each text row are now packed into this unused part of the page memory by modifying the memory address for characters 32 to 39 in each text row. This can be done by using a changeover gate to switch over the row and character lines as shown in *Figure 5.9*. When the character bit for 32 goes to '1' is causes the changeover gate to switch the address lines. Now the 8 and 16 bits of the page memory row address are set at '1' to select the last eight rows in the memory array. The 8 and 16 bits of the teletext row address are now switched to drive the 8 and 16 lines of the memory column address. As a result of

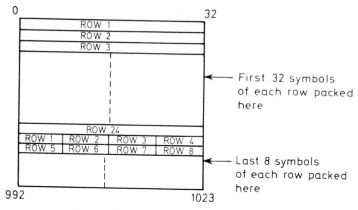

Figure 5.10   Memory packing with a switch control

this switchover the data is written into the memory as shown in *Figure 5.10* and the last eight symbols for each text row are neatly packed into the unused part of the page memory.

In fact it does not matter too much how the page of data is stacked in the memory provided that it is read out in the same order.

Chapter 6

The Text Display

The ultimate aim of any teletext decoder system is to produce a display of the page of text information requested by the viewer. Usually this text will be displayed upon a t.v. screen in place of the normal programme picture.

Some decoders may also have the facility for producing a permanent printed copy of the page of text on a sheet of paper by using an electronically controlled printer unit.

Dot matrix system

The text display will be produced on the screen in much the same way as a normal t.v. picture except that the video signals will now be generated by the teletext decoder unit.

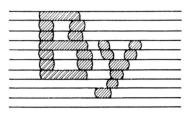

Figure 6.1   Symbols as displayed on a
normal t.v. picture

Consider a normal t.v. picture in which there appears a row of text, such as a title. If the screen area occupied by the text is magnified the image will appear as shown in *Figure 6.1*.

Because of the scanning process used to build up the t.v. picture the row of text will be divided up into a series of horizontal strips as the scanning beam passes over it. In the case illustrated the letters will be relatively small since they take up a screen height of only seven scan lines.

If one scan line through the row of letters is now examined it will be seen to consist of a pattern of black and white dots of varying length. In this case the symbols are made up from black dots against a white background. The corresponding video signal will consist of a pattern of pulses as the scan passes across the row of text.

The size of any text that may be presented as part of the normal t.v. picture may vary widely to suit the composition of the picture. Actual size does however tend to be limited by practical considerations. If the symbols are made smaller than about seven scan lines in height they will not reproduce very well and may become difficult to read. On the other hand using letters more than about 40 lines high will seriously limit the amount of text that can be contained within the width of the picture.

To simplify the design of a teletext display system it is convenient to adopt a standard height for all of the symbols in the page.

In a single field scan of a 625 line picture there are 312½ scan lines of which only 287½ are used for the picture display. Since there are 24 rows of text in the teletext page it is convenient to use 240 lines for the text giving 10 scan lines for each row of text. This will allow some 24 lines at both the top and bottom of the screen for blank margins.

Having decided to use ten scan lines to make up the row of symbols it is convenient to divide up the width of each symbol space in the row into an equal number of dots. This will make the text display look roughly as shown in *Figure 6.2*. Here each symbol space is six dots

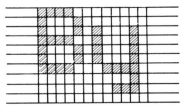

*Figure 6.2   Symbols displayed using a 5
by 9 dot matrix system*

wide by ten lines high. Using this format all of the symbols required for teletext can readily be reproduced by selecting the appropriate patterns of dots within this matrix.

In fact most of the symbols would fit into a 5 × 7 dot area at the top of the character matrix. However some of the lower case letters, such as g, j and y have tails which descend below the main line of symbols. In order to reproduce these letters correctly their tails are allowed to extend down into the eighth and ninth scan lines of the 6 × 10 matrix.

To separate adjacent letters in the row a single vertical column of dots is left blank at one side of the symbol space. Similarly the tenth scan line is left blank to separate the rows of text on the screen.

Character generator

Having decided on a dot matrix display system the next step is to consider how the video signal can be generated. For a start the display generator circuits will need access to all of the dot patterns for the set of symbols to be used. This implies the use of some form of memory device.

One simple scheme for storing the pattern of dots for a symbol might be to use an array of diodes as shown in *Figure 6.3*. Here a

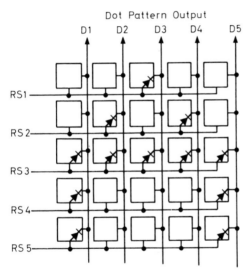

Figure 6.3   Diode array to generate the symbol A

5 × 5 array of dots has been used. Where a dot forms part of the symbol the corresponding cell in the array contains a diode. Each row of cells is selected in turn as the scanning beam moves down the screen. Suppose scan line 2 is currently being displayed. Input RS2 will now be held at say +5 V as the line is scanned.

Any diodes within the row of cells will conduct to drive the corresponding dot output lines to +5V whilst the other dot outputs will remain at 0 V. To produce a video signal the dot output lines are selected in sequence from left to right as the scan moves across the screen. Each dot output line will thus control the brightness of a small segment of the scan line to produce the desired dot pattern.

A simple diode array such as that described will only produce the pattern for one symbol. In the teletext system a set of 96 different symbols may be used. These are shown in *Figure 6.4*. Each symbol in the set is represented by its own unique seven bit binary code in the teletext data signal and these codes are also shown in *Figure 6.4*.

To cope with all of the symbol patterns a large array of diode

				B7	0	0	0	0	1	1	1	1
				B6	0	0	1	1	0	0	1	1
				B5	0	1	0	1	0	1	0	1
B4	B3	B2	B1									
0	0	0	0			Sp	0	@	P	—	P	
0	0	0	1			!	1	A	Q	a	q	
0	0	1	0			"	2	B	R	b	r	
0	0	1	1			£	3	C	S	c	s	
0	1	0	0			$	4	D	T	d	t	
0	1	0	1		Codes	%	5	E	U	e	u	
0	1	1	0		in these two	&	6	F	V	f	v	
0	1	1	1		columns are for	'	7	G	W	g	w	
1	0	0	0		control and are	(	8	H	X	h	x	
1	0	0	1		not displayed	)	9	I	Y	i	y	
1	0	1	0			*	:	J	Z	j	z	
1	0	1	1			+	;	K	←	k	¼	
1	1	0	0			,	<	L	½	l	||	
1	1	0	1			—	=	M	→	m	¾	
1	1	1	0			.	>	N	↑	n	÷	
1	1	1	1			/	?	O	#	o	■	

Figure 6.4   Table of teletext symbols and their associated codes

matrices would be required. Assuming a 5 x 9 dot matrix for each symbol, the inter symbol and inter row spaces being omitted, gives a total of 4320 dot cells. In fact such an array of memory cells is easily built using similar techniques to those used for normal memory devices.

Since the dot patterns for the set of symbols do not change they can be permanently written into the memory array when it is made. Such a memory device provides only the capability of reading out stored data and is called a 'Read Only Memory' or ROM.

When the ROM is manufactured all of its memory cells are identical. Programming of the dot patterns is carried out during the final stages of making the chip. At this point a pattern of wiring links is laid down on top of the array of memory cells and these links determine whether the individual cells are set at '1' or at '0'.

The process used to produce the pattern of links on the chip is similar to that used for making printed circuit boards. A thin layer of metal is deposited on top of the silicon chip and this is then coated with a photosensitive etch resist. Next a photographic 'mask', similar to the negative produced by an ordinary camera, is used to print the pattern of links on to the etch resist layer. Finally the surface is etched to leave a pattern of metal links on top of the memory cells. This type of ROM is called a mask programmed ROM.

Apart from the array of memory cells the ROM will also contain address circuits similar to those used on a random access memory. In this case the address system is usually divided into two parts. Firstly one address using seven binary bits is used to select the pattern of dots for one particular character of the set. This address is arranged to have the same coding as the character code in the teletext data.

A second set of address lines, usually four, selects the row of dots in the character matrix that is to be set up on the memory output lines. This address is used by the display logic to select the appropriate rows of dots in the symbol pattern as the scanning beam moves down the screen.

Finally the outputs from the ROM are brought out to five separate pins so that one complete row of dots is fed out at a time. The output signals are then scanned by the display logic to produce a video signal in the same way as for the simple diode matrix.

A ROM containing these symbol dot patterns in this way is usually called a Character Generator ROM.

Typical character generator

A number of standard character generator ROMs are currently being produced which might be used with teletext. Most of these were primarily designed for use in Visual Display Units (VDUs) associated with computer systems but some were produced specially for teletext use.

One popular ROM in early teletext decoders was the Signetics 2513. This device uses a 5 × 7 dot matrix and provides a 64 character set. The standard version produces upper case letters, numbers and other signs of the ASCII (American Standard Code for Information Interchange) set. Apart from one or two special symbols this is the same set of symbols as that used in teletext and the coding is the same. Unfortunately in order to get lower case letters and some of the other signs a second, differently programmed, 2513 was required.

The first character generator specially designed for teletext use was the Texas Instruments SN74S262 which does provide the complete teletext symbol set. This ROM uses a 5 × 9 matrix to accommodate the tails of the lower case letters. Unlike the 2513, which required three separate power supply lines, the SN74S262 works from the same +5 V supply as conventional TTL logic devices.

Most of the later integrated circuit teletext and viewdata modules have the character generator ROM built into the same circuit chip as the display control logic. These ROMs normally provide the full symbol set, including graphics, and often include a character rounding facility.

Producing the video signal

Having obtained a character generator ROM which will produce on demand those dot output signals corresponding to one row of dots in the selected symbol the next step is to convert these into a video signal. Basically this involves selecting the dot outputs in turn to produce a serial train of pulses. This can easily be achieved by using a shift register as shown in *Figure 6.5*.

The pattern of dots output from the ROM is loaded in parallel to five of the stages of a six stage shift register. The sixth stage is loaded with a '0' state to represent the blank space between adjacent symbols. Now the data is clocked through the register serially. In the diagram the data pattern will move from right to left. At the left hand end of the shift register a serial train of pulses will appear corresponding to the dot pattern and this signal provides the basis for the video output.

Consider now the clock frequency requirements. A line scan period in the 625 line system is 64 μs. Of this time about 51 μs produces the picture display whilst the remainder is used for synchronisation and blanking.

A row of text consists of 40 symbols and a convenient time period for displaying these would be 40 μs giving 1 μs for each symbol space in the line. If there are six dots to each symbol then the dot clock needs to run at 6 MHz. To avoid ragged edges to the symbols this clock must be synchronised to the line scan of the display.

To produce the video signal for a complete scan line the dot patterns for each of the symbols in the row of text must be selected in turn from the character generator ROM and converted into serial pulses.

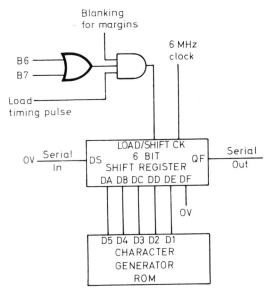

Figure 6.5   Parallel-serial conversion and blanking logic

Figure 6.6 shows the overall block diagram for the display control section of a typical teletext decoder.

At the start of each scan line a monostable circuit is triggered by the line sync pulse. This monostable is used to stop the dot clock and blank the video output to produce a blank margin at the left-hand side of the screen. During this period the first symbol code of the line of text is selected from the page memory and applied to the character generator ROM which then produces the appropriate dot patterns on its output lines. This dot pattern is also transferred in parallel to the six stages of the output shift register.

When the monostable delay period ends the dot clock is started and the pattern of dots for the first character in the row of text is shifted out of the shift register to produce a video signal. At the same time the

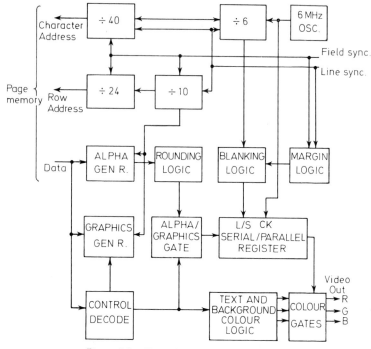

Figure 6.6   Block diagram of display system

symbol code for the next text character in the row is requested from the page memory and its pattern of dots is produced at the output of the character generator ROM. After the last dot of the previous symbol has been clocked out of the shift register the dot pattern for the new character is loaded in parallel to the shift register and then it is clocked out to produce a continuing video output. This process is continued across the line scan until all forty characters in the row of text have been converted into video output.

Character count

In order to keep track of the position of the scan within the row of text a character counter is used. This is a simple six stage binary counter which is arranged to count up from 0 to 40 as the individual symbols in the row are scanned. The six stage counter will, in fact, count up to 63 but a gate is included to detect when the binary output pattern reaches the value of 40. At this point an End of Line signal is generated and this is used to stop the counter and to blank the video signal for the remainder of the scan line to produce a blank margin at the right hand side of the screen.

Since the output of the character counter is a six bit binary code it can be used as part of the address for the main page memory and will cause the symbol codes for each of the characters in the row of text to be selected in turn as the character count progresses. At the start of each scan line the character counter is reset at 0 and will select the symbol code for the first character in the row from the page memory.

A clock signal is needed to drive the character counter. This is derived from the dot clock by taking one dot pulse in every six to produce a short pulse at either the beginning or end of each symbol period in the scan line. This pulse may also be used to load the parallel data from the character generator ROM into the output shift register.

The page memory and character generator devices do not, in fact, produce an output immediately after an address signal is applied. A delay, called the access time, occurs before the output signals become stable. For a typical RAM or ROM device used in teletext this delay is of the order of a few hundred nanoseconds.

To avoid timing problems it is arranged that the character counter, and hence the memory address, is updated immediately after the dot pattern for the current symbol has been transferred from the output of the ROM into the shift register. A period of about one microsecond will be available before the next dot pattern must be transferred and this is ample time for the page memory and character generator ROM to operate.

Line counter

Once the first scan line for a row of text has been completed the row address applied to the character ROM has to be updated so that the next row of dots in the matrix is selected for the following line scan. This row address is derived from a counter driven by the line sync pulses. This counter has four stages giving a count of up to sixteen. A gate circuit is used to reset the counter to zero after ten lines have been scanned so that it will be ready for the next row of text on the page.

During the following nine line scans the page memory is made to select the same sequence of symbol codes for the row of text but the ROM selects a different row of dots in the character matrix for each scan line. On the tenth scan the whole line is left blank to provide spacing between the rows of text on the page.

Row address counter

After the ten scan lines making up a row of text have been completed the row address to the page memory must be updated so that on the next line scan it will produce a new set of symbol codes corresponding to the next row of text on the page.

The row address for the page memory can be produced by a binary counter with five stages. This counter is clocked by a pulse from the line counter at the end of the tenth scan line for a row of text.

At the start of each field scan a delay of about 24 scan lines from the field sync pulse is used to produce a blank margin at the top of the screen. When this delay, which may be produced by either a monostable or by counting line scans, ends the display of the first row of text is commenced. During the margin delay the row address count for the page memory is held at 0 so that the first row of text to be displayed will be row 0 or the header row.

When the row address count reaches 24 it is used to trigger an end of page circuit which stops the dot clock and blanks the video for the rest of the field scan to produce a blank margin at the bottom of the page.

During the field blanking interval, when teletext data is expected, the row and character count addresses of the page memory are switched over to the input logic so that new data can be written into the memory if required.

If a page erasure is required the 'Write' control line to the memory is activated during the display scan and the data input is set to the code for a blank space. Now as the display circuits scan through the memory each location will be overwritten with the code for a blank space to leave a totally blank screen on the following display scan unless some new data is written in. This complete erasure process occurs in one field scan and appears instantaneous to the viewer.

Control code blanking

The seven bit character code for teletext can, in fact, define 128 different symbols although only 96 of these are actually displayed. In *Figure 6.4* the first 32 codes, occupying the first two columns of the table, are shown as blanks. These codes are used by the teletext system for control purposes and must be displayed as a blank space when they occur within a row of text.

Character generator ROMs, such as the SN74S262, will in fact display symbols when these control codes are fed in as the character code. The SN74S262 displays a set of special symbols representing the control codes but some other types of ROM display Greek symbols or some other special set of symbols when fed with these character codes. To ensure proper blanking of these codes the decoder must be able to recognise them and this is easily done because all of the control codes have bits 6 and 7 both at '0'. All displayable codes will have either one or both of these bits at '1'.

A simple system for implementing the blanketing of the control codes is shown in *Figure 6.5*. Here an OR gate fed by bits 6 and 7 of the character code, is used to detect displayable symbols. With either bit 6, bit 7 or both bits at '1' the output of the OR gate is a '1'. This output is used to open an AND gate to allow the parallel load pulse to be applied to the output shift register.

Under these conditions the symbol dot pattern is transferred into the shift register and converted into a video signal. When bits 6 and 7 are both at '0', indicating a control code, the output of the OR gate goes to '0', the AND gate closes and the new dot pattern is not loaded into the register. Normally the serial input to the shift register is set at '0' so that as the dot pattern moves out of the register a series of '0's is shifted in. When the next dot pattern is about to be loaded the shift register will be filled with '0's. If no new dot pattern is loaded the symbol space is displayed as a blank.

Blanking could be achieved by gating the serial dot pattern coming out of the shift register but here a timing problem can occur. The output from the OR gate will go to '0' as soon as the control code appears at the page memory output but this may occur about halfway through the display of the previous symbol and direct gating would result in part of that symbol being blanked. To overcome this the output from the OR gate is clocked into a flip-flop at the same time as the dot pattern is loaded into the shift register. The flip-flop now controls the blanking and will produce the correct timing for the blanking action.

Often the blanking of control codes is combined with blanking for the margins at the top, bottom and sides of the screen.

Character rounding

Although the 5 × 9 dot matrix pattern can produce perfectly legible characters on the screen they can have a rather ragged appearance when there are diagonal or curved lines in the symbol shape. In an effort to produce text symbols with a more attractive appearance a technique known as character rounding may be used to smooth out the diagonal and curved lines.

Normally the dot patterns produced on the alternate interlaced field scans will be identical. On the screen this produces vertical pairs of dots on the adjacent interlaced lines as shown in *Figure 6.7*. It is this line pairing which tends to give rise to the stepped appearance of the symbol on the screen.

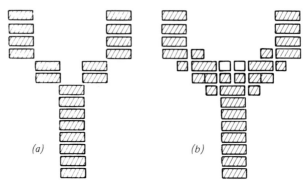

Figure 6.7   *Character rounding (a) Normal symbol display*
(b) Symbol with rounding applied

By modifying the dot pattern slightly on alternate fields these steps can be smoothed out. Here the method used is to add a half length dot either before the normal dot or after it depending upon conditions at the time.

On even field patterns the dot pattern is compared with the pattern on the previous row in the matrix and the half dot is added to partly overlap the dot in the previous row. On odd fields the pattern is compared with that on the next row do determine the position of the half dot.

To carry out the comparison between dot rows two ROMs may be used. The dot patterns of adjacent rows are compared and the required half dot is generated if necessary. If a very fast access ROM is used it is possible to carry out the comparison by accessing the ROM twice for each symbol.

Chapter 7

Graphics and Colour

Apart from the normal display of alpha and numeric text symbols the teletext specification also provides for an elementary form of graphics display. This facility can be used for presenting simple diagrams, such as a weather map, as shown in *Figure 7.1*.

The graphics mode may also be used to produce extra large text characters such as those used for page titles. It is also possible, by using the graphics mode to display quite effective pictures.

Figure 7.1   Weather map page on teletext

Graphics matrix

As in the presentation of text symbols the display area for graphics is divided up into a matrix of dots or segments and these are selectively illuminated to produce the desired patterns on the screen.

Whereas the text symbols use a 6 × 10 dot pattern for each symbol the graphics matrix is much coarser and consists of just six segments as shown in *Figure 7.2*. Now each symbol is made up effectively from two vertical columns of three dots each.

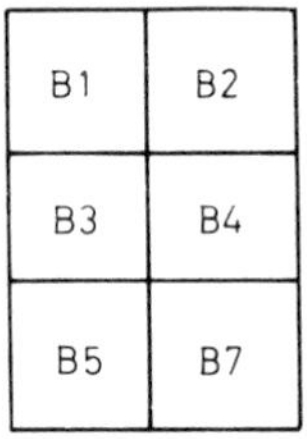

B1	B2
B3	B4
B5	B7

Figure 7.2   The graphics matrix and allocation of bits to the segments

In the graphics mode if we consider the whole screen area there will be an array of 80 dots across the screen and 72 rows of dots down the page. In effect we have a 72 line low definition picture which is rather better than twice the definition of Baird's original pictures and is capable of producing surprisingly good pictures (*Figure 7.3*).

Graphics coding

Since there are only six segments within a graphics symbol space and the character data code contains seven bits, the simplest coding technique is to allocate a data bit to each segment in the symbol space.

When the data bit is set at '1' the corresponding segment in the graphics symbol matrix will be lit whilst if the data bit is at '0' the segment will be left dark. With six segments each of which can be either lit or dark there are 64 different patterns which can be produced in the symbol space. This gives considerable flexibility to the designer producing a teletext page of graphics.

Figure 7.2 shows how the data bits in the character code are allocated to the elements of the graphics matrix. It may seem odd that bit 7 is used for the bottom right hand element. Logically one would expect bit 6 to be used here. In fact, as we shall see later, bit 6 is used to provide a control function when graphics are used and as a result bit 7 has been used in its place in the matrix.

The seven data bits of the teletext character code allow for 128 possible combinations. Of these 96 are used for alphanumeric symbols leaving 32 spare codes. These 32 codes however are required for control purposes. In order to fit in the graphics symbols another 64 codes are required which presents something of a problem. How can the codes for the graphics symbols be catered for?

Consider the operation of a standard typewriter. In its normal mode of operation each key, when operated, will cause a lower case letter or a sign to be printed on the paper. If however the Shift key is operated then each key will now cause a capital letter or a different sign to be printed. This is carried out on a typewriter by literally shifting the position of the type relative to the ribbon and paper hence the term 'Shift key'.

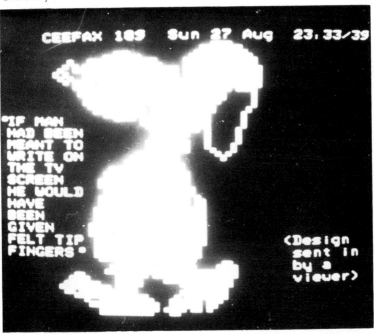

Figure 7.3   A typical graphics picture page

For the graphics symbols a similar Shift operation is used in the teletext system. Here a control code is used to tell the decoder to switch to the graphics display mode so that the following character codes are interpreted as being graphics symbol codes. A second control code is used to return the display to its normal alphanumeric mode. These control codes each take up one symbol space on the screen and these spaces are displayed as blanks.

One might now expect that the first character code in each row of text would be a control code to select the alphanumeric or graphics display mode as required. However this would waste the first symbol space on every text row. Since most pages are likely to be mainly alphanumeric it is arranged in the teletext specification that every row is assumed to start in the alphanumerics mode. Now it is only where the second symbol in the row has to be graphics that a graphic shift code will occur at the start of a row of text.

Figure 7.4 shows the complete set of symbols that can be displayed when the decoder is switched into the graphics mode. Also shown are the various control codes used in teletext to determine the type of display action produced.

				B7	0	0	0	0	1	1	1	1
			B6	0	0	1	1	0	0	1	1	
		B5		0	1	0	1	0	1	0	1	
B4	B3	B2	B1	0	1	2	3	4	5	6	7	
0	0	0	0	NUL	DLE	◻	◳	@	P	◰	◻
0	0	0	1	ALPHA RED	GRAPHICS RED	◩	◪	A	Q	◩	◪
0	0	1	0	ALPHA GREEN	GRAPHICS GREEN	◪	◪	B	R	◪	◪
0	0	1	1	ALPHA YELLOW	GRAPHICS YELLOW	◻	◳	C	S	◳	◼
0	1	0	0	ALPHA BLUE	GRAPHICS BLUE	◳	◱	D	T	◪	◪
0	1	0	1	ALPHA MAGENTA	GRAPHICS MAGENTA	◪	◼	E	U	◪	◻
0	1	1	0	ALPHA CYAN	GRAPHICS CYAN	◪	◪	F	V	◪	◪
0	1	1	1	ALPHA WHITE	GRAPHICS WHITE	◪	◼	G	W	◪	◼
1	0	0	0	FLASH	CONCEAL	◪	◪	H	X	◪	◪
1	0	0	1	STEADY	CONTIGUOUS GRAPHICS	◪	◪	I	Y	◪	◪
1	0	1	0	END BOX	SEPARATED GRAPHICS	◱	◪	J	Z	◼	◪
1	0	1	1	START BOX	ESC	◪	◪	K	←	◪	◪
1	1	0	0	NORMAL HEIGHT	BLACK BACKGROUND	▬	◪	L	½	◪	◼
1	1	0	1	DOUBLE HEIGHT	NEW BACKGROUND	◪	◪	M	→	◪	◼
1	1	1	0	SO	HOLD GRAPHICS	▬	◪	N	↑	◪	◼
1	1	1	1	SI	RELEASE GRAPHICS	◼	◼	O	#	◼	◼

Figure 7.4   Symbol and code table for graphics and control

It will be seen that there are, in fact, a series of seven separate codes which will cause the display to switch to the graphics mode and seven corresponding codes which will switch it back to the normal alphanumerics mode. As will be seen later in this chapter these codes also serve to control the colour of the displayed symbols. They also indirectly control the colour of the background.

For teletext, the codes marked NUL and DLE are not in use and are simply displayed as blank spaces on the page. These codes however may be used with the viewdata systems. To simplify the control logic in teletext these two codes are sometimes treated as graphics black and Alpha Black. Now it can be seen that when bits 4, 6 and 7 are all at '0' then bit 5 will act as the control bit which determines if alpha or graphics mode is to be selected.

Blast through alphanumerics

When graphics and alphanumerics are intermingled in a text row there will need to be a control code inserted each time the display mode is changed. These will produce a series of blank spaces on the screen. It would be useful if the alpha symbols could be displayed within a sequence of graphics symbols without having to change the mode of the display system and hence without the need for control codes. This is where bit 6 of a graphics code comes in.

An examination of the complete symbol table shows that bit 6 will be at '0' only for control codes and capital letters. Suppose now that bit 6 is used to switch the display operation without actually changing the mode. Assuming that the graphics display mode has already been selected any character codes with bit 6 set at '1' will be displayed as graphics symbols as shown in columns 3, 4, 7 and 8 of the table. If bit 6 goes to '0' however then the capital letters and signs of columns 5

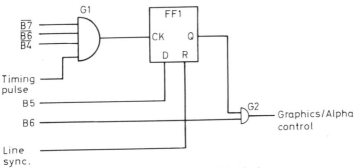

Figure 7.5 Graphics/alpha switching logic

and 6 will be displayed unless the code is a control mode. Since the graphics mode is not actually switched the display will return to graphics on any symbols where bit 6 is at '1'. This mode of operation is referred to as 'Blast Through Alphamerics'.

Figure 7.5 shows a typical logic arrangement for controlling the graphics alpha switching. Bits 4, 6 and 7 are gated to detect a 000 combination and this is used as a clock signal for the mode control flip-flop FF1. Bit 5 is used as the data input for this flip-flop. To ensure proper timing the character pattern transfer pulse from the text generation shift register is also gated with the clock pulse for the flip-flop.

When a graphics mode control code is received the flip-flop will be set with Q at '1'. This signal is now gated with bit 6 to produce the display mode control line. When bit 6 is at '1' the output will be at '1'

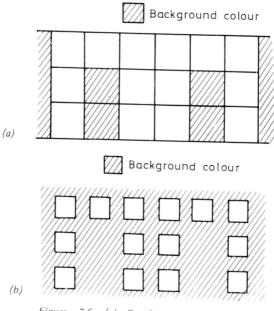

(a)

(b)

Figure   7.6   (a)   Contiguous   graphics   symbols
(b) Separated graphics symbols

and graphics symbols will be displayed. If bit 6 goes to '0' the gate closes and the output line also goes to '0' to produce an alpha display for that symbol. If an Alpha mode control code is received the flip-flop will be reset with Q at '0' and alpha symbols will be displayed irrespective of the state of bit 6. To ensure that the alpha display mode is selected at the start of each row of text the line sync pulse is used to reset the flip-flop at the start of each line.

Contiguous and separated graphics

Normally graphics symbols are displayed with the segments of the symbol touching one another as shown in *Figure 7.6a*. This mode of display is called Contiguous graphics.

During the experimental period the option of using separated segments in the graphics symbols was also tried. This gives a rather different character to the symbols as can be seen in *Figure 7.6b*. The revised specification for teletext caters for both types of graphics symbols by the use of a pair of control codes to select either Contiguous or Separated graphics symbols.

At the start of each row of text contiguous graphics is assumed. If a graphics shift code is encountered then the symbols produced will be of the contiguous type. By inserting a Separated Graphics control code into the text data stream the display mode can be changed and following graphics symbols will be displayed in the separated form. A return to the normal contiguous symbols can be produced by inserting a Contiguous Graphics control code into the data stream.

Some of the earlier decoders do not recognise these new control codes and will therefore display all graphics symbols in the contiguous mode.

Generating graphics symbols

In some of the earlier decoder systems the graphics symbols were generated by means of a simple logic system. Since there are only six segments and each is represented by one of the data bits this is fairly easy to achieve.

Figure 7.7 shows a logic scheme for generating the contiguous graphics symbols. This arrangement was used by the author in an early experimental decoder system.

The individual scan lines making up the row of text are identified by using a divide by ten counter and a one of ten decoder. From the decoder ten outputs are produced one of which will be at '0'. This output indicates which of the ten lines is currently being scanned. The outputs are grouped together into two groups of three successive scan lines and one group of four lines using gates G1, G2 and G3. Unfortunately the ten scan lines cannot be split up into three equal groups but the arrangement shown does produce quite acceptable graphics symbols.

Output signals from gates G1, G2 and G3 correspond to the three vertical segments of the symbol pattern and are fed to a set of six NAND gates (G4 to G9) where they are gated with the six data bits of the symbol code for the graphics character. At the outputs of these gates a signal is produced corresponding to each segment of the symbol pattern to be displayed.

In any particular scan line the outputs from gates G4, G5 and G6 correspond to the first half of the symbol space whilst gates G7, G8 and G9 produce an output for the second half of the symbol space. The

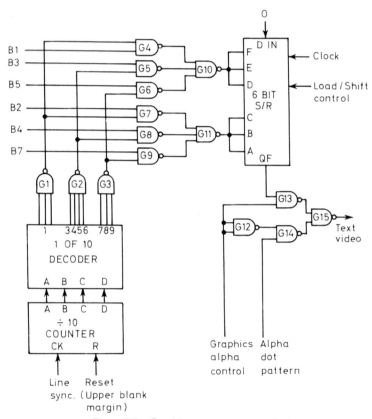

Figure 7.7   Graphics pattern generator logic

outputs from these two groups of three gates are combined together in gates G10 and G11 to produce the drive signals for a parallel to serial shift register which will produce the video output signal for the graphics symbol. This six stage register produces dot patterns in the same way as the one used for alphanumerics symbols. Here the stages are grouped together in threes to form two segments each occupying half the symbol space in the display.

Suppose that only bit 1 of the character code is at '1'. Gate G4 will open during the first three scan lines of the text row setting inputs D, E and F of the shift register at '1'. As a result the first half of the symbol space is illuminated during scans 1, 2 and 3 and the rest of the symbol space will be blank. This produces a single illuminated segment (number 1) in the top left corner of the graphics symbol.

Serial dot patterns from the graphics shift register are combined with those from the alphanumerics character generator logic in a changeover gate system made up from gates G12, G13, G14 and G15. The type of symbol displayed is selected by the Graphics/Alpha control signal derived from bit 6 and the display mode flip-flop.

It is relatively easy to modify this graphics logic to display separated graphics symbols. The segments are separated horizontally by gating the inputs to stages C and F of the shift register. This reduces the segment to two dots in width and leaves a blank dot between each of the segments. By gating the third, seventh and tenth line outputs from the one of ten decoder a single line can be blanked to separate the segments vertically. Control of these gates would be from a flip-flop which is set or reset by decoded Contiguous or Separated graphics commands.

An alternative approach to the generation of graphics symbols is to make use of a Read Only Memory in the same way as is done for the alphanumeric symbols. Here each of the graphics patterns is built up on the same 6 × 10 dot matrix as the text characters. A separate set of graphics symbols can be included to deal with the Separated Graphics mode. If both text and graphics symbols are produced by a single ROM it will need to produce 224 different symbols (96 for text and 64 for each of the graphics sets). This is well within the capacity of modern integrated circuits. For the text symbols the inter character and inter row blank dots will need to be included since the graphics type symbols use the whole of the 6 × 10 matrix.

Most of the modern decoder modules use a ROM to produce the graphics symbols and often this is combined with the rest of the display generation logic to make up a single integrated circuit.

Colour displays

One of the more attractive features of the teletext system is the ability to display the information, either graphics or text, in a range of different colours.

A standard colour receiver uses a colour picture tube having three separate electron guns, one for red, one for green and one for blue. By selectively switching the video drives to these three guns all of the colours required for a colour picture can be reproduced on the screen.

In the teletext system control of the display colour is achieved by allocating one bit of a control code to each of the primary colours red, green and blue. These bits are used to switch the dot pattern drives to the Red, Green and Blue guns of the picture tube to produce the various display colours.

For colour pictures the amplitude of the video drive to each of the three guns can be varied over a wide range to produce all shades of colour. In teletext the video drives will be either on or off depending on the state of the associated colour control bit. This restricts the display to one of seven possible colours. In fact there are eight possible combinations of the three colour bits but one of these has all three bits at '0' and produces black since all three guns of the tube are switched off.

Colour control is combined with the alpha/graphics mode selection and the corresponding control codes occupy the first eight positions in the first two columns of the teletext code table as shown in *Figure 7.4*. It may seem rather wasteful to have two complete sets of colour codes, one for text and one for graphics, but there is some advantage in this form of coding. With other coding techniques a change of both display colour and mode would require a pair of successive control codes, one to change the colour and the second to change the display mode. These will take up two symbol spaces in the row of text. Using the chosen method of coding only one control code is needed to make the change of both colour and mode thus leaving more space for text. This becomes especially important where several changes of colour and mode occur in the same text row.

Bits B1, B2 and B3 of the colour control codes are used to control the red, green and blue signals respectively. When a bit is set at '1' the dot pattern video signal is applied to the appropriate R, G or B gun of the tube. If the colour control bit is at '0' the drive to that gun is switched off.

Suppose the Red control bit (B1) is set at '1' whilst bits B2 and B3 are both at '0'. The display signal is fed to the red gun and a red display results. Bits B2 or B3 at '1' with the other bits at '0' will produce green and blue displays respectively.

If two colour control bits are set at '1' the display colour becomes the combination of the two selected colours. Thus with bits B1 and B2 at 1 whilst B3 is at 0 the display will be yellow (red + green). Bits B2 and B3 together will produce a light greenish blue colour called cyan whilst a combination of bits B1 and B3 will produce a magenta (red + blue) display.

When all three colour control bits are set at '1' the resultant display will be white. Since a large part of the text displayed is likely to be white it is assumed that all rows of text will start off with a white display selected. This avoids the need to insert a colour control code at the start of every text row. After a colour has been selected the change back to white text is controlled by the Text White or Graphics White control code which is inserted in the line of text in place of one of the symbol codes.

Decoding the colour controls

For decoding, the colour control commands a three bit D type latch may be used with one flip-flop of the latch for each colour as shown in *Figure 7.8*.

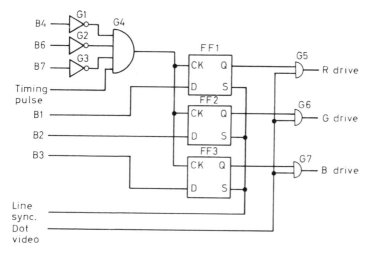

Figure 7.8   Colour decoding logic

At the start of each scan line all three flip-flops are set at '1' by the line sunc pulse thus selecting a white display mode.

Gate G4 is fed by inverted inputs from bits B4, B6 and B7 of the data code and will be active when all three of these bits are at '0'. This gate effectively selects out the group of colour control codes from the table. A short clock pulse is also applied to this gate so that its output will be a short pulse at the start of a symbol space in the display scan. This ensures proper timing of the switching of colour signals relative to the symbol dot pattern.

The output from gate G4 is used to clock the three flip-flops which are fed by bits B1, B2 and B3 respectively at their D inputs. When a colour control code is detected by gate G4 the flip-flops will take up the states of bits B1, B2 and B3 to produce three colour control signals.

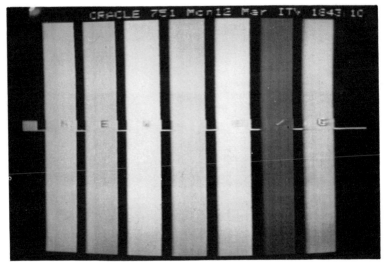

Figure 7.9(a)   Without Graphics Hold

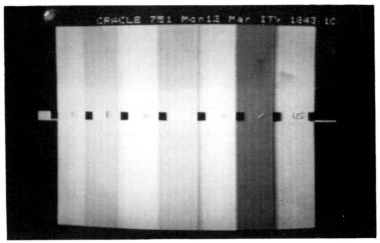

Figure 7.9(b)   With Graphics Hold

These three signals are used to gate the dot pattern video to the three guns of the picture tube via gates G5, G6 and G7 and hence will control the display colour.

Graphics hold

When operating in the graphics mode a change of colour will require the insertion of a control code into the line of text which will result in a blank space being displayed in the graphics pattern as shown in *Figure 7.9a*. A similar effect will occur when any control code is detected. This effect can be avoided by making use of a feature called 'Graphics Hold'.

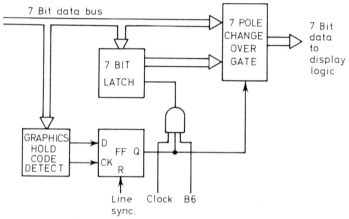

Figure 7.10   Basic scheme for graphics control logic

In the Graphics Hold mode of operation each time a control code is detected the graphics symbol that has just been displayed is repeated so that it fills the blank space that would have been produced by the control code.

Two control codes are used to implement the Graphics Hold feature. Code 001110 selects the Graphics Hold mode of operation whilst code 0011111 returns the display to its normal operation. At the start of every row of text it is assumed that Graphics Hold is not operational.

A basic scheme for implementing the Graphics Hold mode is shown in *Figure 7.10*. Here a separate register is used to hold the code for the most recent graphics symbol detected. When a control code is detected the inputs to the graphics shift register or other form of symbol generator are fed by the code for this previous graphics symbol instead of the control code data that is coming from the page memory. Now a graphics symbol is displayed instead of a blank space.

The code patterns for Graphics Hold and Graphics Release are detected by two gates and used to set or reset a flip-flop which controls the Graphics Hold mode of the display logic. This flip-flop is set to the Graphics Release state at the start of each scan line by a line sync pulse.

If several control codes follow one another in the Graphics Hold mode the blank spaces are filled by repeating the same symbol the appropriate number of times. If there is a 'blast through alphamerics' symbol before the control code the space will be filled by the last graphics symbol code before the alpha character was displayed.

Background colour

In the original specification for teletext the symbols were displayed against a black background. In the revised version however provision has been made for control of the background colour as well as that of the symbols. Thus it becomes possible to display red text on a yellow background.

Unfortunately there are not enough spare control codes to permit direct coding of the background colour so that an alternative technique has to be employed. This makes use of the symbol colour codes indirectly to control the colour of the background.

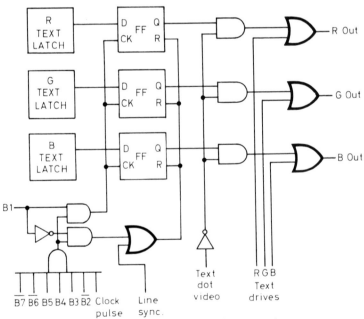

Figure 7.11   Background colour control

Two control codes are used to select the background colour. One is called New Background and has the bit code 0001101. This command causes the background colour to be set to the same colour as the symbols. The second control code for background colour is called Black Background and as its name suggests it causes the background colour to revert to black. Each row of text will start off with the background colour set at black.

If a background colour is set then any control codes will cause the space they occupy to be displayed in the background colour unless the Graphics Hold mode is being used. If the symbol colour is not changed after a New Background command then the resultant symbols will become invisible because they have the same colour as the background. When separated graphics symbols are displayed the spaces between segments are in the background colour as are the normally black parts of a text symbol matrix.

Background control

Figure 7.11 shows a typical logic scheme for decoding and controlling the background colour.

As in the case of the symbol colour control three flip-flops are used to control the background colour. The D inputs of these flip-flops are fed from the outputs of the symbol colour control flip-flops. When a New Background control code is detected it is used to clock the three background colour flip-flops so that they take up the same state as the symbol colour flip-flops. The background will now be the same colour as the symbols.

A Black Background control code or a line sync pulse is used to reset all three background colour flip-flops to '0' thus producing a Black background as required.

The background colour signals are produced by gating the inverted dot pattern from the symbol generator circuits against the three background colour control signals. This background signal is then combined with the symbol colour signal in three OR gates to produce the final Red, Green and Blue drive signals for the display tube.

Now whenever a symbol dot signal is at '1' the tube produces a dot in the display colour whilst if the dot is at '0' the tube produces a dot in the background colour. The margins at the sides, top and bottom of the screen are usually blanked for both display and background colours to produce a black margin around the display.

Decoders which are not fitted with the background colour facility will simply ignore the background control codes and produce the text against a black background.

Chapter 8

Other Teletext Features

Apart from the normal display of pages of text and graphics information in a variety of different colours the teletext system also incorporates a number of other options which can control the display format or increase the total number of different pages of information that can be directly addressed by the viewer.

Boxed operation

One of the original applications envisaged for the teletext system was that of providing subtitles for some viewers without interfering with the normal programme picture being watched by the remainder of the television audience. This facility might, for instance, be used to provide subtitles for deaf viewers or to provide subtitles in a different language. In either case the viewers who wished to see the subtitles would call up an appropriate page in the teletext magazine and have the titles displayed with their pictures whilst other viewers would receive the normal picture without subtitles.

One of the problems which is encountered in making subtitled films for the cinema is that of ensuring that the subtitles are unobtrusive whilst still being easily read. Usually subtitles are inserted at the bottom of the screen area so that they do not interfere with the picture. The second and rather more difficult problem is to make sure that the titles are easily visible against the background produced by the picture itself. Suppose that the letters of the subtitle are white and that they are superimposed upon a light coloured area of the picture. Now the text characters may be difficult to distinguish from the light background and under some conditions will merge into the background and become totally invisible.

During the experimental period of teletext some of the decoders provided a facility for superimposing the text upon the programme picture. This mixed display mode is not however particularly successful for the same basic reasons as the subtitles on a cinema film and also because, since the text on many pages covers almost the whole of the picture area, there was severe conflict between viewing the text and viewing the picture.

One approach to the problem of differentiating the titles from the picture is to blank off a strip of the picture area at the bottom of the screen and to insert the subtitles into the blank space that is produced. The BBC do, in fact, use this arrangement for presenting subtitles for the deaf in some of their news bulletins. Because the text is presented

Figure 8.1   Typical 'boxed' text used for newsflash

against a black background it is easily visible and the only penalty is that a small part of the picture at the bottom of the screen is lost.

Taking this idea a stage further it would be possible to blank out small areas of the picture at any convenient point on the screen and to insert into these spaces some text information. This technique has sometimes been used in sports programmes to display the elapsed time in, say, a race or a football match.

In teletext this process of blanking out areas of the picture and displaying the text within them is used for presenting subtitle and news-flash pages. The blanked out areas are called 'boxes' and the display mode is called a boxed display. Using this approach minimum interference is caused to the programme picture and the inserted text stands out clearly in its box. A typical display of this type is shown in *Figure 8.1.*

Box control

The boxed mode of display is controlled by the use of two control code bytes which can be inserted into the text data stream in the same way as graphics or colour controls. The Start Box code (0001011) causes the picture to be blanked from that point in the scan line and text video is then passed to the display tube. When an End Box command (0001010) is detected the picture signal will be restored and the text suppressed.

When the decoder is operating in the boxed display mode every scan line starts off with the television picture signal selected and at the end of the text area on each line scan the picture is restored whether an End Box code has been received or not.

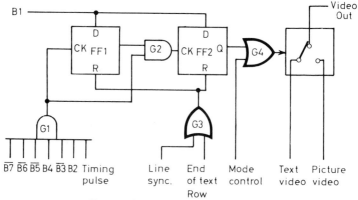

Figure 8.2   Logic for box mode display

To avoid the possibility of spurious boxes being blanked out from the picture the box control commands are sent in pairs. Normally the box should start or end at the end of the symbol space occupied by the first of the pair of box codes. The decoder can if desired check these two successive code words to see that they are identical before opening the box on the screen. There is no timing problem here because the second control code will have been read out from the page memory well before the box has to be opened in the scan line.

A basic logic scheme for implementing control of the box display mode is shown in *Figure 8.2*. Here a pair of flip-flops are used, one controlling the box operation and the second acting as a temporary memory of the previous Box command in the text row.

At the start of the scan line both flip-flops reset and the output control line switches picture video through to the display tube and suppresses the text video. Gate G1 is used to detect any Box commands that occur in the text data. It detects the combination 000101 of bits B7 to B2 coming from the page memory. When a Start Box command is received a clock pulse is applied to flip-flop FF1 and it takes up the state of bit B1. For a Start Box code FF1 will be set by the clock pulse. Flip-flop FF2 is clocked only when the output of FF1 matches the current state of bit B1. At the time the clock pulse occurs FF1 will still be reset so no clock pulse is applied to FF2 and it remains reset leaving the picture signal on the screen.

When the second box code is received, FF1 is already set so this time FF2 will be clocked into the set state and the picture video will be blanked. At the same time text video is unblanked and the text display within the box commences. No further change occurs in the states of FF1 and FF2 until another Box command is received when a similar sequence of events will occur and FF2 will be reset when the second of the pair of End Box codes has been detected. This will close the box and restore normal picture video to the tube.

Selection of the Box mode of display is governed by the OR gate following FF2 which is fed by a control signal called Box Mode. When this control signal is at '0' it has no effect upon the operation of the OR gate and switching of picture and text signals is under the control of FF2 and the Start of End Box codes. If the Box mode signal is set at '1' it will force the output of the OR gate to a '1' state irrespective of the state of the FF2 output. Under these conditions the text mode is permanently selected to give a normal page display of text.

Flashing symbols

Sometimes in composing a page for teletext an editor may wish to draw the viewers attention to some particular item on the page. He can achieve this by arranging that part of the text flashes on and off at regular intervals.

As in the case of Box commands there are two control codes in the text data set which select either flashing or steady symbols. These are shown in *Figure 7.4*.

All text rows commence with steady symbols but when a Flash code is detected the following symbols will flash on and off. To return the text to a steady display state the Steady code is inserted into the data stream. Circuits within the decoder itself will determine the rate at which the symbols flash on and off. This rate must be carefully chosen since some flashing frequencies can be unpleasant or annoying for the viewer.

Decoding of the Flash and Steady commands is carried out in a similar fashion to Box code detection except that for the Flash commands only one command code is sent and takes effect at the start of the next symbol space after that occupied by the control code. A simple oscillator, running at about one cycle per second, is then used to gate the text video to make the symbols flash on and off when flashing symbols are called for. The background is not affected by the Flash command.

Concealed display

One of the ways in which pages in the teletext service have been used is to present questions and answers. This might be used simply for fun quizzes and puzzle pages or more seriously for educational purposes.

In the early days of the teletext service the answers would be presented on a different page from the questions. Sometimes the two pages might be included in a multipage rotating set although this had the disadvantage that it was possible for the viewer to see the answers before seeing the questions. Neither approach gave a satisfactory solution to the presentation of question and answer information.

To overcome this problem it is arranged that parts of the page can be concealed by transmitting a control code called Conceal Display. At the receiving end the viewer is able to choose whether he will see the concealed parts of the page by operating a Reveal button on his decoder. Now the questions are displayed normally but the answers can be blanked off from the display until the viewer decides that he wants to see them.

The control code for Conceal can be detected in much the same way as the Flash and Steady codes. When a Conceal code is encountered in the data stream the rest of the text in that row will normally be blanked on the display. Data is however still written into the page memory so that when the Reveal button on the decoder is pressed the concealed text can be displayed in the normal way. At the start of each scan line the display is set into the normal display mode.

Decoders which are not fitted with the Reveal/Conceal facility will display all text on the page irrespective of any Conceal codes that may be transmitted.

Double height text

Sometimes, in order to make the text easier to read or to emphasise the importance of a particular item, it is useful to be able to display larger than normal symbols.

The graphics mode can be used to display large size symbols and this is regularly done in presenting the page titles. However using graphics requires several symbol codes just to build up one character and is not very efficient if a large amount of text is to be displayed. This problem has been overcome in the teletext specification by including commands which allow text symbols to be displayed with twice their normal height.

Using this double height mode the symbols now take up the space of two rows of text but there can still be up to forty characters in each double height row. As a result if the whole page were displayed in double height about half the normal amount of text could be included.

Two control codes are used to implement the Double Height type of display and these are shown in *Figure 7.4*. One code called Double Height will cause the following text in that row to be displayed with twice the normal height. A Normal Height code can be inserted after some double height text has occurred in a row and this will set the remainder of the text in the row at normal height. At the start of every row of text it is automatically assumed that the display will consist of normal height text.

Generation of the double height symbols is relatively straightforward. If the line count address to the symbol generating ROM is updated only once every two scan lines instead of on every line the dots in the character matrix will each be repeated on a pair of consecutive line scans. Now the symbol will take up twenty scan lines instead of the normal ten and will have twice its normal height on the screen. The symbol width will however be unaltered.

Because the double height symbols take up twenty scan lines the lower half of these symbols will occupy the space where the next row of text would normally be displayed. Thus when double height symbols are included in a row of text that row is treated as if it were a pair of rows and the next row of text data will be ignored.

In order to produce the lower part of the double size characters the data for the text row containing them must be read out of the page memory on twenty scan lines. Thus the row address to the page memory must not be changed until the double height symbols have been completely scanned. At this point however the page memory row address will be out of step with the display and will need to be increased by two to bring it back into step.

When single and double height symbols occur within the same text row the switching between them can readily be achieved by means of a changeover switch feeding the line count address of the character ROM as shown in *Figure 8.3*. For normal height the line count is passed straight through to the ROM but for double height the address bits are mpved one stage up the counter so that the address now changes on every other line scan. An extra flip-flop is added to provide the most

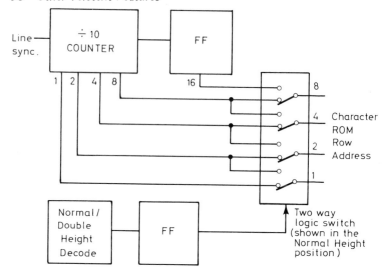

Figure 8.3   Address control for double height switch

significant address bit. This flip-flop is set at 0 during the first ten scan lines of the double height symbols and is changed to 1 for the last ten scan lines. During the second ten scan lines the data for the single height symbols is ignored so that they are displayed as blank spaces.

On a decoder not fitted with the double height mode the symbols are all displayed as single height and if any text data is present on the following text row that will also be displayed.

Time coded pages

The basic system for page selection in teletext allows for eight different magazines of a hundred pages each which gives up to eight hundred directly addressable pages on a single television channel. There may, in fact, be more than eight hundred different pages of text in the transmission but some of these will be in rotating page sets where the individual pages cannot be directly selected by the viewer.

Following the page code bytes in the header there are four bytes allocated to a time code in hours and minutes. Originally it was intended that some pages could be tagged with a time of day code. The decoder could now be arranged to detect this time code as well as the page code and the data for the page would be accepted only when both the page and time codes matched those selected by the viewer.

The general idea of time coded pages was that some pages of information might be transmitted only a few times during the day at certain specified times. Thus we might have say share prices transmitted at every hour then, on the same page number, the exchange rates might be sent at five minutes past the hour and other different pages of information at five minute intervals through the hour. If the viewer wished to see share prices he would select the page number and the time code for the exact hour. Another viewer might set his time code five minutes past the hour and his decoder would accept only the exchange rates page when it appeared in the transmission sequence. If the time code were not used the displayed page would change each time a different set of text was received in much the same way as a rotating page set.

If the page required were transmitted only once a day the viewer could set the appropriate time code and the page would be accepted and stored by the decoder for viewing at a later time. Time coded pages can also be used to produce an alarm clock type operation. Here the viewer merely sets the appropriate time code and when the decoder detects a matching time code in the header row it will grab the data for the page and display it on the screen.

So far the assumption has been made that the time code transmitted in the header row represents the real time of day. During the experimental period it was realised that the time code bytes could be used simply as an extension of the page and magazine address codes. Now a particular page might be identified by a number in the time code which was not the real time of day. This arrangement allows for direct addressing of many thousands of different pages from one transmission.

Time code addresses

Figure 8.4 shows the layout of the four bytes used to transmit the time code in the page header row. Each byte is Hamming coded in the same way as other address information and produces a four bit data code. The time is coded in BCD (Binary Coded Decimal) in the same way as the page number.

In a normal time of day code the Tens of Minutes can only range from 0 to 5 so only three bits are used from this data word. The fourth bit of the Tens of Minutes word is used to control erasure of the page memory when a new set of text is about to be transmitted for the page. Similarly the Tens of Hours word need only have values from 0 to 2 so only two of the data bits are used. The other two bits in this word are used to identify certain types of page as we shall see later in this chapter.

The Tens of Minutes code with three bits can in fact produce the numbers 0 to 7 and the Tens of Hours can range from 0 to 3. Using real time of day coding the minutes will run from 00 to 59 and hours from 00 to 23 giving a total of 1440 possible time code combinations. If the code is merely used as a page number extension then minutes can go from 00 to 79 and hours from 00 to 39 giving a total of 3600 different codes. If this extension were used with all 800 possible page number codes it would be possible to have over two and a half million different directly addressable pages in the teletext transmission.

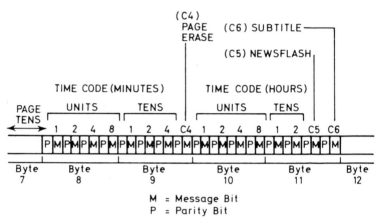

Figure 8.4   Layout of the time code bytes in the Header row

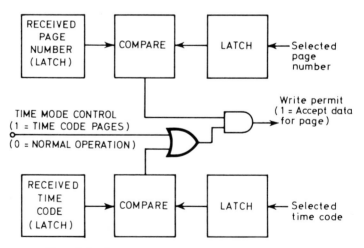

Figure 8.5   General scheme for selecting time coder pages

With only two data lines per field allocated to the teletext signal it is not, at present, practical to send such a large number of different pages. Usually one or two page numbers in the transmission will be allocated for use as time coded pages. To avoid errors in the page display it is usual to transmit each time coded page about four times during its time slot.

Detecting time codes

The basic system for handling time coded pages is shown in *Figure 8.5*. Time code bytes from the header row are detected and stored in the same way as the page address codes. When the time code page operation is desired each time code is compared with the selected code fed in by the viewer. Now the data for the page is accepted only if both the page and time codes match the requested ones.

When the Timed Page mode is not selected in the decoder pages are accepted whenever the page numbers match and the display will be changed as each time coded page is received.

Newsflash/subtitle operation

Pages containing newsflash or subtitle information are normally displayed in the boxed mode where the text is inserted into the normal programme picture. It is possible to have the decoder select the boxed mode automatically for this type of page. This is done by using a pair of control bits in the header row to identify Newsflash and Subtitle pages. These control bits occupy the two unused bits of the Tens of Hours address byte as shown in *Figure 8.4*.

When the first of these bits is set at '1' it indicates that the page being transmitted is a Newsflash page and should be in the boxed display mode. If the second bit is set at '1' it will identify the current page as a subtitle page which must also be displayed in the boxed mode. For all other pages these two control bits are set at '0'.

It may seem unnecessary to use two control bits for this purpose since both types of page use the boxed mode, but there are occasions where the decoder will treat the newsflash and subtitle pages differently and therefore it needs to be able to distinguish one from the other.

Update

When newsflashes are presented on a normal television programme they appear when the news item breaks and may be left on the screen for a minute or two to allow viewers to read them. A similar action can be arranged for newsflashes in teletext. The viewer having read the current newsflash will press a command button labelled Update on his decoder. The screen will now be cleared of text and the programme picture will appear. If the information presented on the newsflash page is changed the new text will be displayed immediately.

This action is achieved by means of a control bit in the header row which informs the decoder that a new page of text is being transmitted on the selected page number. The two address bytes following the Tens of Hours code in the header row are reserved for control and status bits which are allocated as shown in *Figure 8.6*. The second of these control

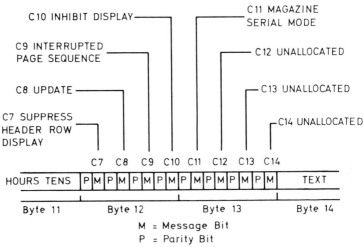

Figure 8.6   Layout of the Control and Status bytes in the Header row

bits is the Update bit which will be set at '1' when new text is inserted on the page. Normally this bit is reset to '0' again after the data for the page has been transmitted once or twice.

Pressing the Update button on the decoder causes any text on the screen to be cleared and the display switched over to picture mode. The decoder will now ignore the data for the selected page unless the update bit in the page header row is set at '1'. When this happens the new page of text is stored in the page memory and display is set back into the text mode.

The Suppress Header bit is used to blank off the header row on some pages, such as graphics pictures, where the page is better displayed without the header row text.

Sometimes in order to give priority to certain pages, such as the index, the page numbers may be sent out of the normal numerical

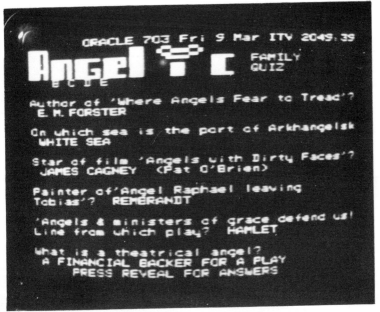

Figure 8.7(a)   Reveal display

Figure 8.7(b)   Concealed display

sequence. If rolling headers are displayed this produces discontinuities in the sequence of numbers which may be confusing to the viewer. A control bit in the header row, labelled Interrupted Sequence, can be set at '1' to indicate that the page is out of numerical sequence and its header row text can be blanked to leave the page numbers in the rolling header in sequence.

Sometimes the text for a page may be meaningless and in these cases a bit labelled Inhibit Display can be used to signal to the decoder that the text is not to be displayed.

Normally all of the text rows in a page are sent out in one uninterrupted sequence. It is possible however to interleave the text rows of several pages to produce an apparent improvement in access time. Here the pages will have the same page code but different magazine codes. Thus row 1 of pages 150, 250 and 350 may be transmitted one after the other then the same sequence would be repeated for the second row of each of the three pages. Because the decoder checks the magazine code at the start of each text row it will accept only the data for the correct page from this interleaved sequence. This mode of transmission is known as Magazine Serial and a control bit in the header row can be used to signal to the decoder that this transmission sequence is being used.

Of the eight available control bits in the last two address bytes of the header row three are at present not allocated although it is possible they may be used in the future to provide some additional facility in teletext.

Chapter 9

Teletext Production

So far in this book we have examined the techniques involved in decoding and displaying teletext. Now it may be interesting to see how the teletext service is handled at the broadcasting centres.

Ceefax

High over Wood Lane in west London, on the seventh floor of the BBC Television Centre, is the editorial suite from which the Ceefax service is controlled.

It is here, in a relatively quiet room away from the bustle of the television studios on the floors below, that a team of journalists compile the pages of text for the two Ceefax magazines. From a corner of the room there is an intermittent chattering as one of the bank of four or five teleprinters types out a news item. These printers provide much of the news information that you will later see on the Ceefax pages. Some printers are linked to news agencies, such as Reuters, whilst others may be collecting information from other departments of the BBC. A printer may be connected to Exchange Telegraph for financial and Stock Market news whilst another may be linked to a sports news service to give the latest racing or football results. Journalists will now take suitable items from these teleprinter machines and edit them to fit into the format of the teletext pages.

Next comes the process of composing the actual page of text that is to be transmitted. This is done by using a typewriter style keyboard which is linked to a computer system in another part of the building. In front of the journalist, as he composes the page, is a colour television monitor which is also controlled by the computer. On this monitor will be displayed the page of text as the journalist builds it up.

Composing the page

Often the journalist will start of by typing in his copy without any commands to select a display colour. This produces a display of white text on a black background. At this stage he is interested in getting the text correct with an acceptable layout of the page. Next he may decide to add a page title with large letters. These extra large letters will be built up by keying in a series of graphics shapes. Sometimes if the title is one that is frequently used the set of graphics patterns will already be stored in the computer memory and the journalist merely keys in a command to insert the stored title into the page of text.

Very often a page that is currently being transmitted in the magazine may need to be edited. A copy of the page is set up in the computer memory and the journalist then alters it by adding or deleting sections of the text to produce an edited version. Whilst this process is going on the page being transmitted is not affected since only the copy in the computer is being altered.

Having composed his page of text the journalist may now key in colour commands to change the colour of parts of the text or he may add some more graphics to improve the appearance of the page. When he is satisfied he will key in a command which tells the computer to insert the new page into the current magazine and within a second or two the new page will go out over the air to the viewers.

The computer

To handle the editing and storage of the pages of text in a teletext service a small digital computer is used. This may well be a minicomputer such as one of the Digital Equipment PDP11 series computers or a similar machine by one of the many minicomputer manufacturers.

Data for the pages of text will usually be stored on a magnetic disk memory which uses a magnetic oxide coated disk as the memory device. As the disk rotates a magnetic head moves radially across it in much the same fashion as the pickup on a record player. Data is written in a series of concentric tracks on the disk and the head moves over the disk to select any desired track to read or write the data. A typical disk may store several million bytes of data, sufficient for several complete teletext magazines.

For editing or transmission, a page of data is read from the disk into the computer's main memory where it is more readily accessible. After editing has been completed the page of data may again be transferred to the disk unit for long term storage. A page for transmission is fed from the computer memory to a teletext encoder where the data is converted into a serial stream and the synchronisation patterns added. The serial data is then inserted into the programme video signal and passed on to the transmitter.

Figure 9.1 shows the general arrangement of the teletext computer

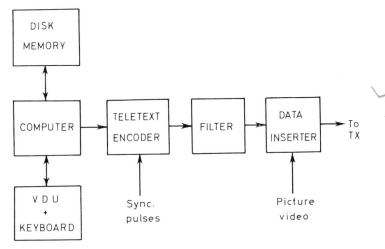

Figure 9.1   Basic Teletext computer system

and editing system. Programs within the computer system, known as the teletext software, control the editing, storage and data transfer processes within the system in accordance with commands keyed in from the journalist's keyboards.

Updating Ceefax

From time to time the information transmitted in the Ceefax magazines is updated. News pages will usually be updated every hour but if some special news item occurs this may be inserted into the magazine as soon as the page has been composed. Some of the other topical pages may be updated two or three times a day.

Pages such as the television programme guide may be changed on a daily basis as would the weather report or a diary of events for the day. Some pages such as the Top Ten pop music chart might be changed once a week whilst a few pages giving such information as postal rates or useful addresses would be changed very infrequently.

At the present time the BBC uses Ceefax 1 which is carried on the BBC1 channel as a form of daily magazine with most of its pages updated on a day to day basis. News is updated more frequently of course. Meanwhile Ceefax 2 on the BBC2 channel acts as a weekly magazine with the contents updated once or twice a week.

Pages on Ceefax 1 are generally numbered from 100 to 199 whilst those on BBC2 have numbers from 200 to 299.

Oracle

The Oracle service on ITV is a bit more complex in its organisation because of the number of independent programme companies that form the network. At present the three programme companies based in London provide between them the pages that make up the current Oracle service.

Independent Television News from its headquarters just north of Oxford Street in London is the source for Oracle pages dealing with news, sport and weather. Here ITN's newsgathering organisation passes on to a team of journalists those items of news to be put in the Oracle pages. The process of editing and composing the text is much the same as that at the BBC Ceefax centre. Once again visual display units and keyboards linked to a computer are used.

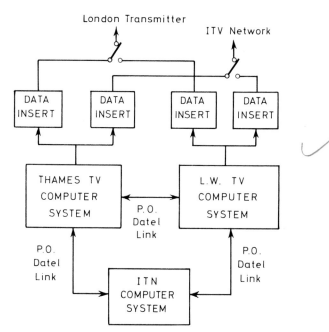

Figure 9.2   The London Oracle network system

A little further north at the Thames Television studios near Euston station a second team of journalists prepare the general interest pages for their section of the Oracle service whilst on the south bank of the Thames not far from Waterloo station a third team of journalists at the London Weekend Television centre put together the remaining pages of the magazine.

To produce the Oracle service all of these different sources of text pages have to be linked together in a network as shown in *Figure 9.2*.

During the week from Monday till Thursday the London areas programmes are produced by Thames Television and all the data for the pages of Oracle generated by ITN and London Weekend are routed through to the computer at the Thames Television centre. From this computer the data for all of the Oracle pages is then added to the programme video signal and sent out to the London area transmitters. At the same time the signal is also sent out to the other ITV stations around the country via the ITV network.

At weekends when London Weekend take over the London area programming the Oracle signals from Thames and ITN are transferred to the LWT computer for insertion into the ITV network and for transmission via the London stations. Data is transferred between the three computer systems by means of a Post Office data line.

Data bridges

In the early days of the Oracle service the text was only broadcast from regional stations when they were transmitting a programme networked by either Thames TV or London Weekend TV. At this time there was no means by which these local stations could inject the text signals into their own programmes.

To overcome this problem and to make Oracle available to regional viewers devices known as Data Bridges were made and installed at the major regional studios. These units made use of the fact that most of the regional centres had a video signal feed coming from the London programme even when they were transmitting their own local programmes. In the data bridge Oracle signals from London are decoded retimed and then inserted into the local video signals.

The block diagram of a typical data bridge is shown in *Figure 9.3*. Video signals from the London programme company are received from the ITV network and fed into a data slicer after which the teletext signals are gated out in much the same way as in a normal teletext decoder. The Framing code is detected and teletext data is converted into the parallel format and written into a small memory. This memory

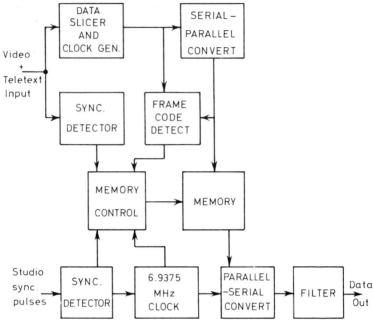

Figure 9.3   Block diagram of data bridge

will probably hold about four rows of the text data at a time. Magazine and row address data is stored as well as the text information.

Sync signals from the local television programme are then used to lock a 6.9375 MHz oscillator and to control the reading of data from the store. Text data is now read out word by word and converted into a serial bit stream, using a shift register, and then passed via a filter to a data insertion unit which adds the text signals to the local programme. The clock run-in and Framing code for the locally generated signal are also transferred as fixed bit patterns into the parallel—serial shift register at the start of each of the data lines so that the inserted data signal is the same as if it had been generated completely at the local centre.

Oracle magazines

Unlike Ceefax where one magazine number is used for all of the pages on a channel, the Oracle service makes use of some pages in nearly all of the magazines from 100 up to 899.

Magazine 2 consisting of pages 200 to 299 is used by Independent Television News and covers national and world news, sport, finance and business news. Page 250 is usually reserved for newsflashes.

Magazine 7 on pages 700 to 799 is a consumer magazine with pages covering fashion, records, books, hobbies and even horoscopes. Magazine 3 is generally used for news about the regional stations of the ITV netowrk giving details of local programmes, local events and perhaps local news. Some of these pages are compiled by the local network stations but inserted into the magazine in London.

Magazine 5 is the London magazine covering news and events in the London area. Magazines 1 and 6 tend to be used as general magazines. Often magazine 1 is used for special pages whilst magazine 6 tends to be for children and also carries educational pages for schools.

Some pages may carry advertisements either using the full page or inserted at the bottom of another page of text. Pages have been used to transmit pictures ranging from a simple cartoon to portraits of famous people.

Updating of the Oracle pages varies with their content in much the same way as the pages in a Ceefax magazine and in general the policies on the two services tend to be similar in this respect.

As the use of teletext expands, the variety of news and information presented will increase although the number of pages is likely to remain about the same until more data lines are used because of access time limitations.

Chapter 10

Viewdata

The second type of text information service which is available to the British public is the Post Office Prestel service which uses the viewdata system where data is sent via the public telephone network. Originally viewdata was the name chosen by the Post Office for their information service but this was later changed to Prestel and the term viewdata, like teletext, is used to describe the system of transmission used to provide the service.

In many respects the teletext and viewdata systems are similar since they both use television displays to present the pages of text whilst the page format and data coding for the two systems are virtually identical. The major differences are in the techniques used to transmit the data signals and to select the page of text which is to be displayed.

Teletext is basically a one way communication system in which the complete set of pages of text is transmitted at frequent intervals using data signals carried as part of the broadcast television programme. The only control available to the user is that he can select which particular page from the received set his decoder will accept, store and display. The need to repeat continuously the whole set of pages tends to limit the total number of pages to one or two hundred. With more pages the time needed to go through the whole set of pages and hence the access time for any particular page becomes unacceptable.

Unlike teletext, the viewdata system does provide a two way communication link between the user and a viewdata centre. Now the desired page can be requested by sending a command signal directly to the computer at the local viewdata centre. This command is decoded by the computer and the data for the selected page is then transmitted to the user and may be stored and displayed in much the same way as for a teletext page.

Because only the data for the selected page is sent to the user, the data transmission rate can be relatively low thus allowing the signals to be sent over a standard telephone circuit. At the same time the response from the computer is virtually immediate since it can start sending data for the selected page as soon as the requested page number has been decoded. Because there is no need to send data for the whole set of pages it now becomes possible to provide an enormous data base containing perhaps millions, or tens of millions, of pages. Whereas teletext provides the user with an electronic newspaper the viewdata system provides the equivalent of an electronic reference library.

Viewdata network

The general arrangement of a viewdata information network is shown in *Figure 10.1*. Normally the individual user will dial and gain access to a viewdata centre in his local telephone area. As a result his telephone

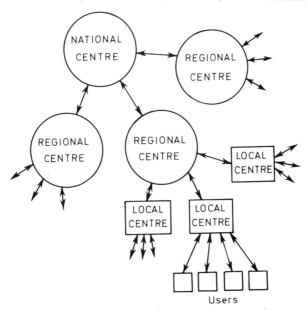

Figure 10.1   Typical arrangement of a viewdata network system

charges will be for a local call. The local viewdata centre might have available some 50 000 pages of information including perhaps a wide range of local interest topics.

If the requested page of information is not among those available at the local computer an automatic link is made to a regional viewdata centre and the required page of data is transferred from the computer located there. This regional centre might give the user access to perhaps half a million pages of text including any local interest items from the other local computers that are located within the region. From the regional centre a further link can be made to a national centre which will give users access to data bases throughout the country. This principle could be extended further to provide a worldwide network by linking national centres together via cable or satellite links.

Much of the information for viewdata will be fed in by commercial organisations who will pay a fee for using the viewdata system. In return however they may make a charge for access to the information they have supplied. In these cases the access fee will usually be indicated on the page itself and in the viewdata index. The user will normally be charged for the telephone call at normal local rates and in addition may have to pay a small charge for computer time in accessing a page. These charges together with any charges for viewing a page of text will be made in the same way as for normal telephone calls and the fees for use of the information will then be passed on to the firms that supplied the information.

In many ways the operation is very much like that of a large library where most of the information is free but some special items are charged for to cover the cost of providing the service.

Using viewdata

Let us now see how a viewer, with a suitably modified television receiver, might actually use the viewdata system. The first stage in the proceedings is to pick up the phone and dial the local viewdata centre. When the connection is made the computer at the centre will respond by sending a 1300 Hz tone. At this point the viewdata decoder unit must be switched into the data mode and it will send out a signal to the computer indicating that it is ready to accept data.

The computer will usually request an identification signal from the user to which the viewer will reply by sending his own unique identification number as a code of up to 16 decimal digits. This allows quite a number of users to be individually identified so that the correct user can be charged for the use of the service. Once the identification procedure has been satisfactorily completed the computer will send data for the first page of data which will then be displayed on the viewer's screen. This page will usually be page 0 which is the master index page for the viewdata system.

One aspect of viewdata which required some careful consideration was the need to have a system which would be easy for the ordinary man in the street to operate. There are already many computer-based information systems in use but generally these have relatively complex operating systems. In viewdata the number of commands has been cut to a bare minimum and the method of selecting a desired page has been made self-explanatory once page 0 has been shown on the screen.

On page 0 the user is presented with a list of nine options, numbered from 1 to 9, and is invited to select one of them by keying in the appropriate number on his control unit. Some of these options will be 'magazines' covering various different types of information, such as business, home or general interest items, whilst other options may select some of the special services available to viewdata users.

When the user keys in a number it is encoded and sent to the viewdata computer which responds by sending data for a new page of text. This new page will perhaps present a further set of ten choices, numbered 0 to 9, for the user. On selecting one of these the computer will respond with yet another page and so on until the user eventually gets the particular page of information he is seeking.

The page selection process uses a tree type system where each step provides up to ten different choices as shown in *Figure 10.2*. As an

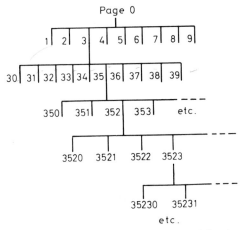

*Figure 10.2   Typical tree structure used for view-
data page selection*

example, if the user takes 3 as his choice from the page 0 options he will then have page 3 presented on the screen. If he now chooses option 5 from the new page the computer will respond by sending page 35. If the next choice is 2 then the next displayed page will be number 352 and so on. As the viewer moves down the selection tree the subject matter presented will become more specific and the information more detailed. After perhaps eight selection steps the displayed page number might be 35265841 and might give details of perhaps the menu for a restaurant in Birmingham.

As an example of the page selection process the user might first choose a general interest magazine. At the next step he might choose say Entertainment and then continue down the tree selecting Theatre, London Theatres, West End Theatres and finally say the London Palladium. At this point he might be presented with details of the shows to appear at the Palladium for perhaps the next eight weeks. Going further it might be possible to obtain details of individual shows for example.

In a similar way one might choose Sport, then Golf, local clubs and so on until perhaps a page has been reached which gives details of the green fees, course layout or perhaps details of individual holes on a selected golf course. The major advantage of this type of selection scheme is that the user can move from page to page without needing an index or a complicated page selection process.

Viewdata commands

Apart from the numbers 0 to 9 the viewdata control keyboard has two further keys labelled ✳ and #. In some decoders the teletext Page and Update keys may be used for these functions. There are only four basic commands which are needed to operate the viewdata page selection process.

After a time the user may become familiar with the numbers of pages that he frequently refers to and he may not wish to work his way down the selection tree every time he wishes to view one of these pages. He can in fact select the desired page directly from page 0 by keying in the sequence ✳ *n* #, where *n* is the number of the desired page. So for page 357 the user would enter the command ✳ 357 #.

Having found a desired page and read it the user may wish to return to the main index page (page 0). This can be achieved by using the command sequence ✳ 0 # which causes the page 0 display to be restored to the screen.

Whilst working his way down the selection tree a user may accidentally select the wrong number for the next page. This situation can be remedied by keying in ✳ # which will cause the previously displayed page to be presented again. The user can now make his selection again.

Errors may occur from time to time in the transmission of data for a page so that the resultant display becomes incorrect. By using the command sequence ✳ ✳ the user can make the computer send the data for the current page again. This command may also be used as a REDO command for some of the other viewdata facilities.

Row	B4 B3 B2 B1	Col 0	Col 1	Col 2	Col 2a	Col 3	Col 3a	Col 4	Col 4a	Col 5	Col 5a	Col 6	Col 6a	Col 7	Col 7a
		000	001	010		011		100		101		110		111	
0	0 0 0 0	NUL		Sp	▪	0	▪	@	NUL	P	DLE	—	▪	p	▪
1	0 0 0 1		DC1	!	▪	1	▪	A	ALPHA RED	Q	GRAPHICS RED	a	▪	q	▪
2	0 0 1 0		DC2	"	▪	2	▪	B	ALPHA GREEN	R	GRAPHICS GREEN	b	▪	r	▪
3	0 0 1 1		DC3	£	▪	3	▪	C	ALPHA YELLOW	S	GRAPHICS YELLOW	c	▪	s	▪
4	0 1 0 0		DC4	$	▪	4	▪	D	ALPHA BLUE	T	GRAPHICS BLUE	d	▪	t	▪
5	0 1 0 1	ENQ		%	▪	5	▪	E	ALPHA MAGENTA	U	GRAPHICS MAGENTA	e	▪	u	▪
6	0 1 1 0			&	▪	6	▪	F	ALPHA CYAN	V	GRAPHICS CYAN	f	▪	v	▪
7	0 1 1 1			'	▪	7	▪	G	ALPHA WHITE	W	GRAPHICS WHITE	g	▪	w	▪
8	1 0 0 0	BS	CANCEL	(	▪	8	▪	H	FLASH	X	CONCEAL	h	▪	x	▪
9	1 0 0 1	HT		)	▪	9	▪	I	STEADY	Y	CONTIGUOUS GRAPHICS	i	▪	y	▪
10	1 0 1 0	LF		*	▪	:	▪	J	END BOX	Z	SEPARATED GRAPHICS	j	▪	z	▪
11	1 0 1 1	VT	ESC	+	▪	;	▪	K	START BOX			k	▪	¼	▪
12	1 1 0 0	FF		,	▪	<	▪	L	NORMAL HEIGHT	↓	BLACK BACKGROUND	—	▪	‖	▪
13	1 1 0 1	CR		-	▪	=	▪	M	DOUBLE HEIGHT	↑	NEW BACKGROUND	=	▪	¾	▪
14	1 1 1 0		CURSOR HOME	.	▪	>	▪	N		←	HOLD GRAPHICS	n	▪	÷	▪
15	1 1 1 1			/	▪	?	▪	O		#	RELEASE GRAPHICS	o	▪	█	▪

COLUMNS 2a, 3a, 6a, 7a produced after Graphics select code
COLUMNS 4a, 5a produced after ESC code

Figure 10.3 Complete viewdata code table

Viewdata coding

For compatibility with teletext the symbol codes and the colour, graphics, etc, control codes are basically the same as for teletext as shown in *Figure 10.3*.

There is one important difference however concerning the position of the colour, graphics and other teletext type control codes. In standard data communications systems the codes in the first two columns of the code table are used for a series of control functions. In order to make viewdata compatible with other data systems and with computers these control codes must be retained. As a result the teletext display control codes have been moved to columns 4 and 5 of the code table and are selected by means of a shift coding system.

When one of the teletext display control codes is to be transmitted via viewdata it is preceded by the Escape (ESC) control code. This ESC code tells the decoder system that the following data byte is not a symbol code but one of the teletext display control codes. Usually a decoder will simply invert bit 7 of the following symbol code if it encounters an ESC code. The result of this action is to change the display control code to its proper code pattern before it is written into the page memory. This ensures that the proper display action will be produced. Control codes in columns 0 and 1 of the table when received via viewdata are dealt with separately.

Cursor controls

A second fundamental difference between teletext and viewdata is in the method of addressing the memory when data is to be written into it.

In teletext each row of text is identified by a row address code transmitted at the start of each data line. In viewdata a cursor system is used to address the page store.

The cursor shows the position of the symbol space in the page memory that is currently being addressed for writing data into the memory. It may be displayed on the screen as an underline in the particular symbol space on the screen display or by a cross hatch pattern superimposed upon that symbol space. A series of control codes in the viewdata system allows the position of the cursor to be moved around the display to any desired symbol position.

When the computer is about to send a new page it will first transmit a Form Feed (FF) control code. This sends the cursor to the top left hand corner of the page display and causes blank spaces to be written into every memory space. This produces a blank screen in much the same way as the Erase command does in teletext. The memory address for the write mode is now set at character 0 and row 0 ready to accept the new page of text.

As symbols are received and written into the memory the cursor and hence the memory address moves along by one character position at a time. At the end of each row the character address returns to 0 and the row address will be incremented so that the next symbol appears at the start of the next row down the page.

The cursor can be moved without writing symbols into the page memory by means of the cursor control commands. Horizontal Tab (HT) and Backspace (BS) allow the character address to be increased or decreased by one which moves the cursor right or left by one space respectively. Line Feed (LF) and Vertical Tab (VT) perform a similar function on the memory row address thus moving the cursor down or up the page one row at a time.

Two further commands are Carriage Return (CR) which sets the cursor back to the start of the current line by resetting the character address of the memory to zero, and Home which sets the cursor back to the top left hand corner of the page without erasing the display.

The cursor does not always have to be displayed on the screen and a pair of control codes may be used to switch the cursor display on or off as desired. Command DC1 causes the cursor to be displayed whilst DC4 turns the cursor off. If the cursor is turned off the memory address will still be controlled by the cursor commands and data will be written into the appropriate memory locations.

Signal coding

Viewdata uses the asychronous Start/Stop method of transmission with a 10 bit code. The code pattern consists of a start bit, seven data bits for the symbol code, the parity check bit and one stop bit as shown in *Figure 10.4.*

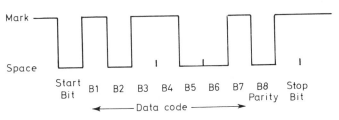

Figure 10.4   Asynchronous data for viewdata showing the code pattern for the letter M

For transmission from the computer to the user the data rate is 1200 bits per second giving 120 characters a second. Thus a complete page takes about 8 seconds to send. Because blank rows and blank spaces at the end of rows need not be transmitted an actual page may take only some three or four seconds to transmit. The display itself can be seen to build up on the screen as the data is received.

Signals from the user's keyboard are transmitted to the computer at the much slower rate of 75 bits per second or 7.5 characters per second. This is the lowest standard data transmission rate but operates much faster than the user can press the keys.

Modems

The actual logic signals of the serial data cannot be transmitted directly along the phone lines so they are turned into audio frequency tones with one tone frequency for the Mark level and another for the Space signal.

For the 1200 bit per second signals the Mark tone is 1300 Hz and the Space tone is 2100 Hz. At the 75 bits per second data rate a tone of 390 Hz is used for Mark and 450 Hz for a Space. During the idling periods the 1300 Hz and 390 Hz signals will be present on the telephone lines and these signals are detected at each end of the line to indicate to the decoder and computer that communication has been established.

The audio tones are generated and detected by a MODEM (Modulator-Demodulator) unit at each end of the phone line. For modulation two separate oscillators, one for Mark and the other for Space, may be used to generate the tones and the appropriate tone is switched on to the line under the control of the data logic signal.

An alternative approach is to use a voltage controlled oscillator where the data signal is used to provide the control voltage and the signal levels are adjusted so that the oscillator output switches between the two required tone frequencies in sympathy with the data signal. Demodulation uses an f.m. detector to convert the received tones into two voltage levels which are in turn amplified to produce the required output logic signals.

The modem unit at the user end may either be built into the viewdata decoder or television receiver or it may be a standard Post Office data communications modem unit as used for connecting computer systems together.

To protect the telephone network from possible high voltages that might be present in the TV receiver, the signals from the modem unit are passed through a barrier isolation unit before being fed in to the phone line itself. This unit allows the speech and audio tone signals to pass but blocks any high voltages which might damage equipment within the telephone network.

Viewdata decoder

The memory and display sections of a viewdata decoder are virtually identical to those in a teletext decoder (*Figure 10.5*). It is in the input circuits for the page memory that the main differences occur. The

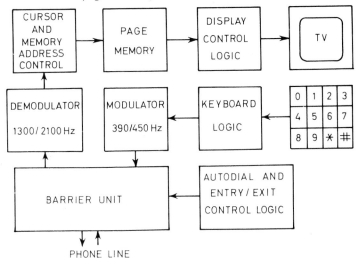

Figure 10.5   Block diagram of typical viewdata decoder

memory character and row addresses are generated by two counters whose operation is governed by the cursor commands. These two counters must be capable of counting either forwards or backwards and may also be reset by cursor commands.

The cursor codes are detected in the decoder unit and used to generate appropriate control and clock signals for the address counters so that the data will be written into the proper position in the page memory. The memory is usually eight bits wide with the eighth bit being normally at 0 but set at 1 in the memory location corresponding to the cursor position. This 1 bit from the eighth bit of the memory is used to control the generation of the cursor display on the screen.

Autodialling

The process of dialling the viewdata centre and making a connection to the computer is usually fully automatic in a viewdata decoder. The

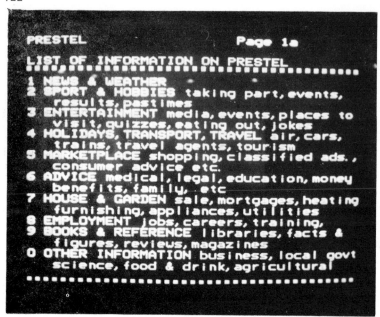

Figure 10.6   Viewdata page selection sequence (1)

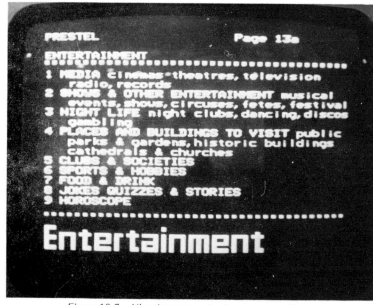

Figure 10.7   Viewdata page selection sequence (2)

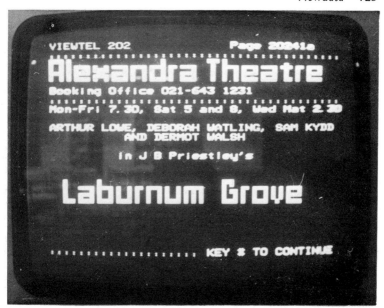

Figure 10.8   Viewdata page selection sequence (3)

pattern of pulses needed to dial the local viewdata centre is stored in a Read Only Memory. Often there will be three or four different phone numbers stored in this ROM and the user will simply operate a switch to select the desired number.

On pressing a key, possibly labelled Viewdata Entry, the user can initiate the complete sequence of entering the viewdata system. Firstly the decoder will send out the sequence of dialling pulses and on receipt of the 1300 Hz tone from the computer it will automatically switch to the data mode and send out its own 390 Hz Mark tone to establish communication with the computer. On receipt of an ENQ code from the computer the decoder will reply by sending its own unique identification code. After this the computer sends data for page 0 and this will be displayed to show that the user is able to use the viewdata system. A similar automatic technique may also be used to sign off from the viewdata system.

Chapter 11

Typical Decoder Systems

Although the early experimental teletext or viewdata decoders used large numbers of standard digital integrated circuits nearly all present-day and future systems will use modules made up from specially developed large scale integrated circuits.

In this chapter we shall examine the systems developed by four major semiconductor manufacturers and also look at some typical receiver systems.

Tifax (Texas Instruments)

The first specially designed module for decoding and displaying teletext to go into production was the Tifax XM11 unit manufactured by Texas Instruments Ltd. In this module several specially designed integrated circuits were used to replace the mass of 74 series TTL devices used in the earlier decoders. As a result the size was greatly reduced and construction and installation were made much simpler.

An XM11 module consists of a small printed circuit board (160 mm × 100 mm) on which are mounted fifteen integrated circuits. Apart from some simple interface circuits to match the XM11 into the particular television receiver being used and a keyboard for control of teletext functions, the XM 11 provides a complete teletext decoding and display control system. *Figure 11.1* shows the basic system diagram of the XM11 module and the module itself is shown in *Figure 11.2*.

A linear integrated circuit using a high speed wide bandwidth bipolar technique provides the data slicer, data clock and synchronisation circuits. The data slicer itself is a fully adaptive arrangement which sets up a mean slice level based on the peak white and black levels of the video with a further correction derived from the amplitude of the teletext data itself. Output signals from the slicer are at normal TTL signal levels.

Also included on the chip is a voltage-controlled oscillator for the data clock and the line and field sync pulse separators.

A logic circuit using the low power Schottky TTL process carries out the detection of the framing code and the serial to parallel data conversion.

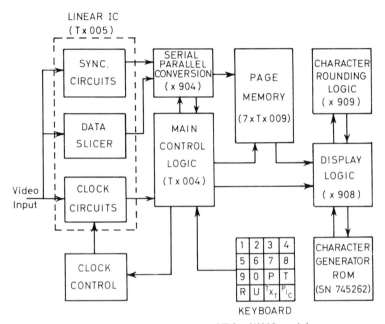

Figure 11.1   Block diagram of Tifax XM11 module

Another Schottky TTL circuit is used for control of the data clock VCO and generates all of the other timing signals needed within the decoder system. This device has the divide by 444 circuits and phase detectors needed to produce the correct clock frequency of 6.9375 MHz and to synchronise this properly to the display scan and the incoming data.

One of the largest integrated circuits on the module board is used to perform all of the housekeeping functions of the unit. Here the Hamming code error checks are carried out and signals from the control keyboard are decoded and used to select the required page of text data from the incoming data stream. Here a relatively new fabrication technique, called Integrated Injection Logic (*I²L*) has been used to meet the speed requirements and to accommodate all of the signals needed a 40 pin DIL package has been used.

Figure 11.2   Tifax XM11 teletext module

Display system

The second large integrated circuit, also in a 40 pin DIL package, contains the display control logic. Internally this chip is arranged as shown in *Figure 11.3*. Data from the page memory is checked for control codes and these are decoded and used to control the display mode as necessary.

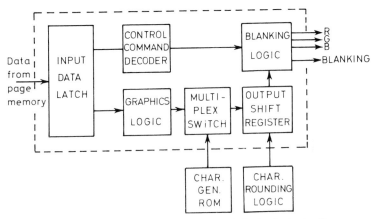

Figure 11.3   Block diagram of X908 display logic circuit

Dot pattern data from the character generator ROM outside the chip is fed to a parallel-serial register which produces the output video signals. These signals are gated with the colour controls to produce the red, green and blue outputs.

Graphics generation is carried out by logic within the display chip and the appropriate dot pattern data is switched to the output shift register in place of the alpha symbol patterns when the graphics mode is selected.

For character generation the SN74S262 type ROM is used together with a special chip for character rounding. In this arrangement the ROM is read twice during each of the symbol scan periods. Firstly the current row of dots to be scanned is read out and then the preceding or the following row of dots is read according to whether the display scan is for an odd or even field. The two rows of dot data are stored in the rounding chip and appropriate half dots are generated as required by the rounding logic.

In the XM11 module the graphics hold and separated graphics symbols are not implemented. Other facilities not catered for are background colour and double height symbols so the decoder will ignore all commands for these display modes and substitutes black background, single height and contiguous graphics displays.

Installation of the XM11 module into the television receiver involves extracting a video signal from the IF or video sections of the receiver and feeding the R, G and B outputs plus some blanking signals to the R, G, B amplifiers in the receiver. Actual interface circuits and techniques will vary according to the design of the TV receiver being used. Power for the Tifax module can be derived from the receiver power supply circuits in most cases.

A calculator style keyboard is used to control the operation of the Tifax module. Usually there are 16 keys connected in a 4 x 4 matrix. Strobe pulses from the XM11 select columns of keys and the four row outputs are fed to four input pins on the Tifax module. Decoding of the particular key operated is carried out in the XM11 itself. Keys labelled 0 to 9 are used to insert page and time code numbers whilst other keys select the functions Page, Time, Picture, Text, Mix, Update and Reveal. In the Mix mode the text is displayed as white symbols superimposed on the programme picture. Some receivers will use an ultrasonic remote control system where a 5 bit serial code is often used to convey commands to the receiver. Here a decoder is used in the receiver to match the ultrasonic commands to the Tifax module requirements by converting the five bit code into a set of signals similar to that produced by a keyboard unit.

For viewdata a variation of the XM11 system called the VDP11 may be used. This module contains a total of 31 integrated circuits and to accommodate these a larger, 300 mm x 165 mm, circuit board has been used.

Teletext decoding and display control are catered for by the basic XM11 system but access to the memory is provided to allow viewdata information to be inserted in place of normal teletext data. A TMS9980 microprocessor based system is used for the decoding and control of the viewdata signals. An autodialling facility is included with up to three telephone numbers stored in a PROM. To interface the VDP11 to the telephone line a modem or line coupling unit will be required. When the VDP11 is used for viewdata outside normal television hours it will generate its own sync pulses to control the display circuits of the television receiver.

Figure 11.4 shows a typical VDP11 module.

Tifax system 12 (Texas Instruments)

Since the introduction of the XM11 and VDP11 modules Texas Instruments have developed a second generation series of modules for teletext and viewdata which they have called System 12.

To simplify updating of existing receivers the XM12 module has

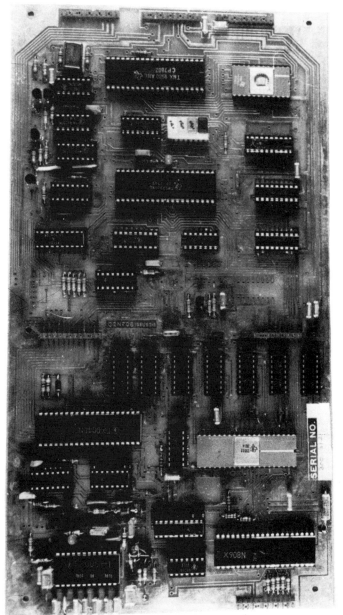

Figure 11.4 *Texas Instruments VDP 11 viewdata module*

been designed to be compatible with the earlier XM11 unit. By using more LSI devices and newer types of memory chip the total number of integrated circuits in the XM12 has been reduced to six. All of the display control, including the character generator ROM, is included in one chip, the TX121. A second chip (TX123) provides all of the teletext decoding whilst a third (TX122) controls system timing. Two 1024 × 4 bit memory chips make up the complete page memory whilst a single linear circuit for the slicer, clock and synchronisation sections complete the complement of integrated circuits. This new module provides all of the display features currently required for teletext.

A second teletext module, the M12, incorporates a number of extra features including Hold Page, Expand Page and the use of up to four separate pages of memory. Where several pages of memory are used each page may be loaded or displayed at will by commands from the keyboard. The Hold feature is useful when viewing a set of 'rotating' pages since it allows the current page display to be held on the screen until the viewer has finished reading it. In the Expand mode either the top or bottom half of the page may be expanded, using double height text, to fill the conplete screen. This makes for ease of reading the text display from a distance.

In the VDP12 viewdata module a TMS29940 microprocessor system is used to control the operation in the viewdata mode. For teletext and display control this module has the circuits of the M12 built in. By extra programming it would be possible to use this module for other activities such as the control of TV games, automatic selection of TV channels at preset times or possibly for use with a personal computer system.

Mullard teletext decoder

In their approach to teletext Mullard have adopted a slightly different technique to that of the XM11. Here most of the integrated circuits use the MOS process and for the production module only eight are used. *Figure 11.5* shows a block system diagram for the Mullard teletext module.

Video signals are processed by a bipolar type linear circuit called the SAA5030 Video Input Processor. This has an adaptive data slicer to ensure minimum data errors. The circuit also contains two clock generators. One clock is used for system timing and display control using a 6 MHz crystal controlled oscillator whilst the second runs at 6.9375 MHz using a pulsed LC tuned circuit and provides a clock for decoding the incoming data. The tuned circuit and crystal are both external to the integrated circuit.

An adaptive sync separator is used to provide the sync pulses for the decoder system. When running from a normal TV signal these pulses are derived from the video input but in the absence of a video signal the sync pulses are derived from the display timing circuits to allow the unit to operate outside normal television broadcast hours. The changeover of sync signals is automatically carried out if the video input disappears.

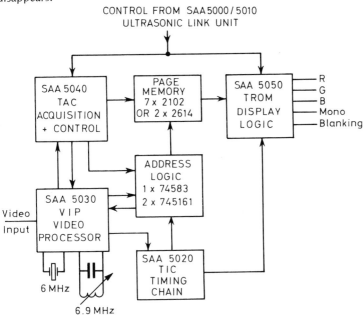

Figure 11.5   Mullard teletext decoder block diagram

A novel feature of the SAA5030 is a signal quality detector which allows the display to free run and cuts off the teletext data input if the video signal becomes too noisy. This prevents corruption of data that may already be stored in the page memory.

The second special LSI circuit is the SAA5040 which uses NMOS technology and carries out the data selection processes. Here the serial data is converted into parallel format for transfer to the page memory and the Hamming coded words are detected and corrected. The selected page and time codes are stored in this chip and used to select the appropriate page of text from the incoming data stream. The SAA5040 also generates the row address and write permit signals for the page memory. A Write Address Clock signal is also fed to the memory section and this allows the character address to be incremented after each character data code has been written into the memory.

The control bits in the page header row are detected in this integrated circuit and appropriate display action, such as Erase Memory, Update, Newsflash, Subtitle, etc is taken.

Timing for the display system is derived from the 6 MHz crystal clock by a complex divider chain contained within the SAA5020 Timing Chain integrated circuit. Here the symbol clock, display character count, row address, character line address and even composite sync pulses, for after hours use, are derived from the basic 6 MHz clock input. The basic arrangement of this chip is shown in *Figure 11.6*.

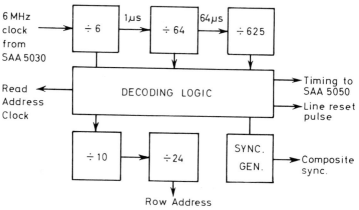

Figure 11.6   Block diagram of the SAA5020 timing chain

In prototype versions the memory section consisted of seven 1024 bit static RAMs with two 74S series counters and an adder to provide the address control. In production versions a pair of Signetics 2614 RAMs (1k × 4 bit) will be used instead of the original 2102 type RAMs. The address system uses a pair of 74S161 binary counters to generate the character address and the adder provides correction to pack the data into the 32 × 32 memory array.

For the display system an SAA5050 circuit is used. This device contains the character generator ROM and the graphics generation logic. It detects control codes and takes the appropriate display action giving the full set of teletext display facilities. Character rounding logic has been included to produce improved symbol appearance. A parallel to serial shift register within the chip gives the serial dot pattern signals which are then gated with the colour controls to produce the Red, Blue and Green video outputs. In addition monochrome and blanking outputs are provided.

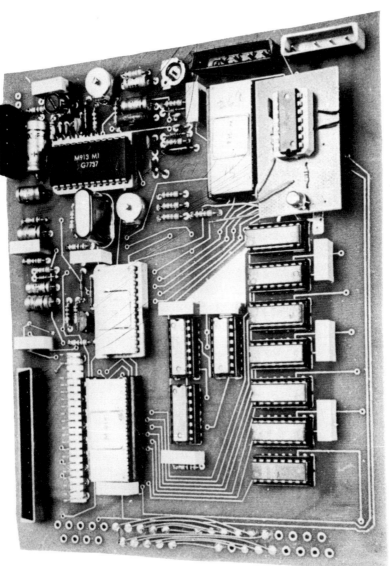

Figure 11.7   Prototype version of Mullard teletext unit

Remote control

The Mullard teletext decoder module was specifically designed to work with a Mullard remote control system using the SAA5000 control encoder and SAA5010 receiver decoder. A five bit command code allows for thirty two different commands which may include control of volume, contrast, brightness, TV on/off and channel selection as well as a full range of commands for teletext.

Signals from the SAA5010 are passed via a common bus line to both the SAA5040 and SAA5050 to control selection of pages and the various display options.

The SAA5000 takes signals from a keyboard with up to 32 keys and converts them into a serial pulse train for the ultrasonic transducer used as a transmitter. At the other end of the link, signals from a receiving transducer are amplified and fed to the SAA5010 decoder. The serial code includes protection against spurious signals that may be picked up by the receiver transducer.

Apart from its use with ultrasonic transmitters and receivers the remote control system may also be used with an infra red transmission system.

When viewdata operation is required an additional module based on a Signetics 2650 microprocessor system is used. Signals from a telephone line are passed through a line coupling unit and into the viewdata module where the microprocessor carries out decoding and processing of the data. For teletext operation and the production of a display the basic circuits of the teletext module are used. In the viewdata mode the memory data and address lines are driven by the viewdata unit instead of the teletext input circuits. The line coupling unit is provided as a separate module and contains facilities for autodialling of viewdata telephone numbers.

In the Mullard system teletext pages are selected by simply keying in a three digit page number, or seven digits for time coded pages, and the requested page number will be displayed at the top left of the displayed page. The header row now turns red and displays rolling headers until the new page has been detected. Whilst searching for the new page the display will continue to present the last page. On receipt of the new page data the old display is erased and the header returns to its normal colour as the new page of text is written on to the screen.

A command called Large Top, or Large Bottom, may be used to expand a half page of text to fill the whole screen for distant viewing in much the same way as the Expand Page mode of the later Tifax decoders. The Mullard unit also has a Page Hold facility for use with rotating page sets.

Teleview (General Instrument Microelectronics Ltd)

General Instruments have based their Teleview system on the use of a microprocessor and two specially developed large scale integrated circuits. Unlike the other manufacturers GI are primarily concerned with making and supplying the special integrated circuits rather than complete ready built teletext/viewdata modules. This leaves the equipment manufacturer with the freedom to design his own printed circuit boards to suit his own needs and to match the engineering practice used for the rest of his equipment. This policy has worked very effectively with GI's range of special integrated circuits for television games.

The overall arrangement of the GI Teleview system is shown in *Figure 11.8*. Each of the major sections of the decoder can communicate

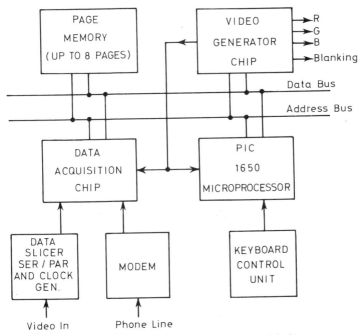

Figure 11.8   Block diagram of General Instrument Teleview system

with other sections via an 8 bit data bus and a 14 bit address bus. Each chip is allowed access to the common bus system at certain times during the display scan and at these times it may receive or send signals to other chips in the system.

From the point of view of timing the key chip in the system is the Video Generator integrated circuit which controls the display of the page of text. An externally generated 6 MHz clock, phase locked to the incoming video signal, provides the basic timing clock for the system. As 6 MHz it forms the dot clock for generating the output video signals. Inside the Video Generator chip it is divided to 1 MHz to produce the character clock and then further divided to produce a composite sync signal if the incoming video signal fails. Normally a composite sync signal from the incoming video is applied to the Video Generator chip to synchronise the text display to the television picture signal for 'boxed' operation in the teletext mode.

Two control signals generated by the Video Generator and called TS1 and TS2 are used to control access to the data and address busses by the other chips in the system. During the period when the text display is being scanned this chip takes control of the address bus to call up data from the page memory.

The display circuit contains a character generator ROM and graphics ROM as well as all control decoding needed to implement all of the required display facilities. At the output Red, Green and Blue signals are available together with a Video On/Off signal which will control switching between text and picture video signals in the TV receiver.

For data acquisition a second specially designed IC is used which is called the Data Acquisition chip. Unlike the other teletext modules the GI system does not include the data slicer and data clock regeneration circuits so these have to be built external to the Teleview system. The input requirements for the Data Acquisition chip are a seven or eight bit parallel data input and a strobe pulse to tell the IC that data is present at the inputs.

During the scan lines where teletext data is to be expected the Data Acquisition chip takes control of the data and address busses. The Hamming coded data signals are processed to give the page, magazine and row addresses and these are compared with the requested page number which is stored in a register within the chip. When the correct page is detected data is written into the page memory.

Addressing of the page memory is in straightforward numerical sequence from 0 to 959 and the arithmetic to convert from row address and character count is carried out within the Data Acquisition chip.

Also included in this chip are two small random access memories used for command and status information. The input RAM contains eight four bit words which are used for the page number and time codes. Data from this RAM is compared with that in each header row to see if the correct page of text is being received. When the page is detected a flip-flop is set to control acceptance of data for that page. The second RAM contains four four bit words and is used to transmit status information to the microprocessor. The state of each of the control bits in the header row may be interrogated in this way.

Control processor

A PIC1650 type microprocessor chip is used to give overall control of the Teleview system and allows the user to communicate with the Data Acquisition and Video output chips. During the period following the teletext lines and before the first line of text is displayed (lines 23 to 47 and 336 to 360) the microprocessor takes control of the data and address busses. During this period it is able to load page and time codes into the data acquisition chip and check the state of the control bits received in the last header row. It is also able to send data to the video chip to control the display.

Signals from a keyboard or remote control system can be fed to the microprocessor to control selection of the page number, display state etc this being determined by the programme used with the processor.

For viewdata operation the signals from the phone line are first of all converted into parallel data signals with a strobe pulse in the line transmission unit. These signals are then applied to the data acquisition chip in place of the teletext signals. A control command from the PIC1650 is used to switch the operation of the data acquisition chip to the viewdata mode. A cursor is displayed by writing a 1 into the appropriate memory byte using bit 8 of the page memory which is not normally used for text data.

In the viewdata mode the text data is written into the memory only during those lines where teletext data is normally expected. To avoid possible timing problems a first in first out memory containing four words is used to hold the text data until it can be written into the memory. The various control operations in the viewdata mode are governed by the microprocessor programme.

The three integrated circuits forming the basis of the teleview system use NMOS technology and run from +5 V and +12 V supplies.

GEC system

The fourth of the semiconductor manufacturers who are producing teletext/viewdata devices is GEC Semiconductors Ltd.

GEC have produced a series of building block modules from which teletext and viewdata systems can be assembled. Each module uses specially developed large scale integrated circuits to reduce the number of devices in the module.

Central to the GEC system is a Self Displaying Page Store which contains just four integrated circuits as shown in the block diagram of *Figure 11.9.* Here the display itself is controlled by the MA400 chip which contains the character and graphics generators, control decoding and display logic. For the page memory two MA414 1024 × 4 bit static RAMs are used and the address logic is contained within the MA401. An 11 bit address bus giving row and character count is used.

To produce a teletext decoder two more integrated circuits and a few discrete components are added to the Self Displaying Page store. An MA403 analogue circuit is used for the data slicer and clock regeneration. The clock uses a pulsed tuned circuit which is mounted external to the integrated circuit. Page detection and all other logic for teletext input control is contained in the MA402 IC. The decoder and display

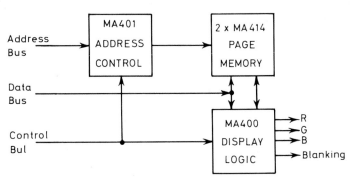

Figure 11.9   Block diagram of GEC self-displaying page store

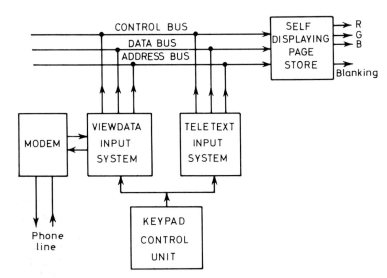

Figure 11.10   Block diagram of GEC viewdata unit

can be obtained as a single board module giving full teletext functions and control from a simple keypad control unit.

For viewdata operation GEC have produced a control module which is used in conjunction with a Self Displaying Page Store to produce a viewdata system. If this module is combined with the teletext decoder module a complete teletext/viewdata system can be produced. The block diagram of such a system is shown in *Figure 11.10*.

Apart from its use for teletext or viewdata the Self Displaying Page Store can also be used to provide a TV display for a microprocessor based games package or a home computer system. It may also be used to interface a teletext viewdata system to record pages on a cassette tape recorder.

CM7026 Colourtext (Labgear)

One of the first teletext units to become generally available to the public was the Labgear Colourtext adapter. Unlike other teletext systems, which are designed to be built directly into a television receiver, the Colourtext is a stand-alone unit that can be used with any unmodified television receiver.

The basic principle used is shown in *Figure 11.11*. Inside the adapter is a complete TV tuner and i.f. amplifier system which provides the

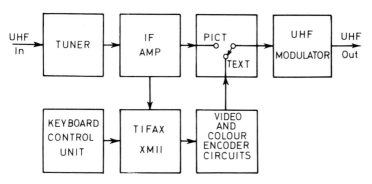

Figure 11.11 Block diagram of Colourtest adapter

video signal for teletext operation. This video signal is decoded by a Tifax XM11 module which produces the appropriate display video at its output. The signal is used to produce a modulated u.h.f. signal on one of the unused channels and this signal is fed to the television receiver which will deal with it as if it were just another TV station.

Hence a text display can be produced without modifying the TV receiver. For colour operation the R, G, B signals from the Tifax unit must be encoded on an internally generated subcarrier in the adapter. Sound from the TV programme may also be added to the output u.h.f. signal if desired. When the box mode is used the combined picture and text signal is used to modulate the u.h.f. carrier.

Due to limitations in the response of the chrominance channel of the domestic TV receiver when an adapter is used for coloured text the colours will usually be less saturated than those that can be obtained by direct video drive to the R, G, B amplifiers of the receiver. The adapter does however provide a useful means of receiving teletext on an already available set.

Teletext receivers

A number of television receivers featuring a built-in teletext decoder have appeared on the market from the British television manufacturers. In many cases these receivers use the latest chassis and are often the top of the range set.

From Thorn the first production teletext receiver was the Ferguson 3782 Colourstar which uses the Thorn 9600 type chassis and features a 26 in precision in line gun tube. For teletext, a Tifax XM11 module is used although in later versions this is likely to be replaced by the XM12 to give the full teletext facilities.

Remote control is provided for both teletext and the normal receiver functions and this uses a 28 channel ultrasonic type system.

Rank also use the Tifax module for their Arena type receivers fitted with teletext. Here the remote control is usually by means of a wire link to a calculator style keyboard unit.

In their receivers using the CVC30/2 and CVC32/2 chassis ITT also use a Tifax module for teletext. Again remote control uses an ultrasonic system designed by ITT. For viewdata operation however ITT use their own design decoder and control system.

Philips receivers use the Mullard teletext decoder system which is understandable since Mullard are part of the Philips organisation. Pye receivers are also likely to use the same system for teletext. Here the ultrasonic remote control by Mullard is used to match the decoder.

The model C2639 receiver from GEC features both teletext and viewdata facilities. The decoder system, as one might expect, uses GEC Semiconductors modules and for viewdata the modem or line terminating unit is built into the receiver and complies with the isolation requirements of the Post Office for equipment connected to their lines.

Remote control uses an ultrasonic system and the receiver is also equipped to handle inputs from video recorders.

As when colour was first introduced many viewers are likely to rent their first teletext receiver since a typical receiver with teletext may cost about 50% to 70% more than the equivalent standard model. Several of the rental companies such as Multibroadcast and Radio Rentals do in fact have teletext equipped receivers available for rent at charges which are some 50–60% higher than for an equivalent size colour receiver.

Viewdata is likely to be used mainly by business users rather than home viewers and for this purpose some special viewdata terminals are available either on rental or for outright purchase.

Chapter 12

A Look into the Future

At this point it might be interesting to emulate the ancient Greek priests by attempting to gaze into the future to see how teletext and viewdata might develop.

It is likely that in the home of the future the TV receiver will no longer spend its entire working life in displaying television pictures. Already, with a widespread use of TV games units the television set is used purely as a display system for the game. As receivers for teletext and viewdata become more widespread we shall see many home television sets displaying text rather than pictures for at least part of the day. Another more recent development has been the home computer system, using a microprocessor, which in many cases will also use the television set as a display system.

Teletext

As the number of viewers equipped to receive teletext increases the most likely development in the teletext services will be an increase in the number of pages and the range of topics covered by the magazines. With only two data lines per field allocated for teletext however the present magazines have already come close to the limiting number of pages beyond which access times become unacceptable. This situation can only be improved by allocating more of the blank lines for carrying teletext data which will allow magazines to increase to maybe 500 or even 1000 pages each.

Multipage rotating page sets are at present usually limited to a set of perhaps three to five pages so that the whole set can be repeated reasonably frequently. In future the number of pages in such a set may increase to perhaps forty or fifty and each page would carry a time code for identification so that the viewer could select any page in the set for display. This technique might be used for such items as election results, or sports results.

Teletext could be used for educational purposes and some experiments in this direction have already been tried. Here teletext might be used to carry the teacher's notes which at present are usually in printed form.

With the advent of home computer systems an interesting possibility for teletext is to broadcast computer programs or data on some pages. This data might either be copied by the viewer and entered into his computer by hand or could be fed directly into the computer system. Thus we might get not only the receipe of the week but also the computer game or other program for the week. Many of the latest TV games are also based on the use of microcomputers and it seems possible that new games data or programs could be broadcast via teletext.

On the international scene teletext has already begun to spread and at the time of writing teletext services are already running on an experimental basis in Australia, Sweden and Holland whilst several other countries are getting ready to start experimental services using the British teletext system as a standard. In some cases the symbol set has been modified to allow for special accented symbols used in the local language.

Viewdata

Initially the Prestel viewdata service provided by the British Post Office started with three regional centres at London, Birmingham and Ipswich. As the service expands, more regional and local centres will be added until the service covers the entire country. National centres in England, Scotland and Wales might then be set up and it is possible that these, in turn, might be connected to other national centres around the world. As each new centre is added to the network it will bring with it a new series of information providers and consequently a range of new pages of information.

It is possible that, apart from the Prestel service, other independent viewdata services might be set up which would use the public telephone network but be controlled independently of the Post Office Prestel service.

Messages and electronic mail

Viewdata, with its two way link between the user and the viewdata centre, can provide facilities that cannot be dealt with by broadcast teletext services. One of these is the possibility of one user sending a message via viewdata to another user. The sender would need an alpha-numeric keyboard rather than the normal twelve key unit used for the basic viewdata service. Having typed in his message he will key in the identification number of the user to whom he wishes to send the message. At the viewdata centre the message will be stored in the computer memory.

When a user enters the viewdata service he will normally be asked for his identification number and following this he will be told if there are any messages waiting in store for him. By keying in appropriate numbers he will then be able to call up to the screen each of the messages and when he has finished with them they will be erased from the computer memory.

This basic idea could perhaps be extended from the simple two or three line message to allow several pages of text to be sent to another user. Now the system provides what is effectively an electronic mail service especially if printed copies of the pages can be produced to give a permanent copy of the message.

Another possible development using the two way link capability of viewdata is the provision of an electronic shopping service. In this case the user might select either a particular shop, assuming that it subscribed to viewdata, or the type of merchandise he wished to buy. On the displayed page he might be given the option of one or two different items and would be asked to indicate how many he wished to purchase. After this the system would ask for a credit card or bank account number to which the goods must be charged. To protect the customer he would now be asked for his own personal password or number before the sale would be completed. Assuming all was in order the goods would be charged to his account and the store would be told where to deliver them unless they were to be collected.

Provided adequate security, in the form of passwords or numbers, has been included in the system it would now be possible to carry out all kinds of personal or financial transaction without moving from the comfort of one's own armchair. Business meetings and conferences could be held using viewdata with the individual participants spread all over the country, or even over the world. This could lead eventually to large numbers of people working from their homes rather than commuting to an office in the city. One disadvantage of holding con-ferences by viewdata, from the point of view of the participants, is that the social side of the conference, such as personal contact, enter-tainment, good food and the prospect of a few days away from home, would be missing which might make the idea rather unpopular in some circles.

Sometimes viewers may wish to have copies of certain pages of teletext or viewdata in much the same way that they might cut interesting items out of newspapers. This could be achieved either by recording the data for the page on say a cassette tape or by using some form of hard copy device such as a printer. To record data it would be read out of the page memory relatively slowly and converted into serial format similar to that used for viewdata. The logic signals would then be converted into tones by a modem and these would be recorded on a standard audio cassette recorder. To recover the page the tape is simply played back through the modem and the data treated in much the same way as if it had come via viewdata.

Appendix

Glossary of Terms

Access time. The time between selecting a page at a receiver and the first complete reception of that page.

Alphanumerics character. One of the 96 display characters. The shapes of the characters are not defined but they should all be different and recognisable.

Alphanumerics mode. The display mode in which the display characters are those of the alphanumerics set.

Alphanumerics set. The set of 96 display characters comprising all the alphanumerics characters.

Background colour. The colour filling the parts of the character rectangle not occupied by the character itself. The background colour may be black or one of the seven display colours. It may be changed within a row by control characters.

Boxed mode. The display mode in which, under the user's control, the characters are intended to be inset or added to a television picture. When a newsflash or subtitle is transmitted this operation may be automatic under the control of control bits.

Broadcast teletext. The information broadcasting system.

Byte. A group of eight consecutive data bits intended to be treated as an entity.

Character byte. The byte obtained by appending an odd-parity bit to a character code.

Character code. A seven-bit binary number representing one of a set of display characters, or a control character.

Character rectangle. One of the 960 units in the regular matrix of 24 rows of 40 sites in which characters are generated in the display of a page.

Character row. See Row.

Clock run-in. A sequence of alternating bits at the start of a data-line to allow a receiver to achieve bit synchronisation.

Conceal. A display mode during which all characters, although stored in the receiver, are intended to be displayed as spaces until the viewer chooses to reveal them.

Contiguous graphics set. The set of 96 display characters comprising the 64 contiguous graphics and 32 of the alpha symbols, together with the 32 blast-through alphanumerics characters.

146

Contiguous mode. The display mode in which the six cells of the graphics characters fill the character rectangle.

Control bits. Each page-header contains 11 control bits to regulate the display of the page and its header.

Control character. One of the 32 characters listed in columns 0 and 1 of the code table. Five of these are reserved for compatibility with other data codes. The others are used to alter the display modes. They are usually displayed as spaces.

Data-line. One of the otherwise unused lines of the television field blanking interval used to carry information for one teletext character row. A data-line is identified by the clock run-in sequence followed by a framing code at the appropriate time on a line in the field interval.

Display character. One of 222 different shapes which can be generated in a character rectangle as part of a page. There are alphanumerics characters to provide text, and graphics characters to provide elementary pictorial information. There are three sets, the alphanumerics set, the contiguous graphics set and the separated graphics set, each of 96 display characters, some of which are common.

Display colour. One of the seven colours (white, yellow, cyan, green, magenta, red, blue) used to depict a display character against the background colour in a character rectangle. The display colour may be changed within a row by control characters.

Display mode. The way in which the character codes corresponding to display characters are interpreted and displayed depends on display modes established by previous control characters. These modes may be changed within a row, and an initial set of modes is defined for the start of a row.

Flash. A display mode in which the characters are blanked out at regular intervals under the control of a timing device in the receiver to produce a blanking display.

Framing code. A byte following the clock run-in sequence, selected to allow the receiver to achieve byte synchronisation even if one of its bits is wrongly decoded.

Graphics character. One of 127 different display characters based on the division of the character rectangle into six cells, the cells being contiguous or separated. The corresponding character codes have $b_6=1$; there is a direct correspondence between the other six bits of the code and the states of the six cells of the character rectangle.

Graphics mode. The display mode in which the display characters are those of one or other of the graphics sets, depending on whether the contiguous or separated mode obtains.

Graphics set. See contiguous graphics set and separated graphics set.

Hamming code. In the teletext system a hamming code is a byte containing four message bits and four protection bits. A single bit error in such a byte can be corrected. Hamming codes are used for sending address and control information.

Hold graphics. A display mode in which any control character occuring during the graphics mode results in the display of a held graphics character.

Magazine. A group of up to a hundred pages, each carrying a common magazine number in the range 1—8. Up to eight magazines may be transmitted in sequence or independently on a television programme channel.

Newsflash page. A page in which all the information for display is boxed, and control bit C_5 is set to allow this information to be automatically inset or added to a television picture.

Page. A group of 24 rows of 40 characters intended to be displayed as an entity on a television screen.

Page-header. A page-header data-line has row address '0' and it separates the pages of a magazine in the sequence of transmitted data-lines. In place of the first eight character bytes it contains hamming coded address and control information relating to that page. Thus the corresponding top row of the page has only 32 character bytes. These are used for the transmission of general information such as magazine and page number, day and date, programme source and clock time.

Release graphics. The display mode in which control characters are invariably displayed as spaces. It is complementary to the hold graphics mode.

Reveal. The display mode complementary to the conceal mode.

Rolling headers. The use of the top row of the page to display all the page-headers of the selected magazine as they are transmitted. This gives an indication of the page transmission sequence while the user is watching, or awaiting, a selected page.

Row. A page comprises 24 rows of characters. When displayed on a television screen each row occupies about 20 television display lines. Each row is generated from the information on one television data-line. It is to avoid confusion with television 'lines' that teletext pages are said to contain 'rows'.

Row-adaptive transmission. Teletext transmission in which rows containing no information are not transmitted. This reduces the access times of the system. The non-transmitted rows are displayed as rows of unboxed black spaces.

Separated graphics set. The set of 96 display characters comprising the 64 separated graphics characters corresponding to the contiguous graphics characters together with the 32 blast-through alphanumerics characters in columns 4 and 5 of the code table.

Separated mode. The display mode in which there is a background colour boundary around and between the six cells of the graphics characters within the character rectangle.

Space. A character rectangle entirely filled by the background colour.

Subtitle page. A page in which all the information for display is boxed, and control bit C_6 is set to allow this information to be automatically inset or added to a television picture.

Television data-Line. See Data-line.

Time-coded page. In addition to a magazine number and page number a page may be assigned a 'time code' of one of 3200 numbers arranged as two 'hours' digits and two 'minutes' digits. This code may be used to select one of many pages, bearing the same magazine and page number, transmitted in sequence. When the transmission of each version of the page is isolated or infrequent, this code may be made literally the 'hours' and 'minutes' of the clock-time at which it is transmitted.

Time display. The last eight characters of every page-header are reserved for clock-time. A receiver may be arranged to display these characters from the rolling headers to give a clock-time display.

(Reproduced by courtesy of the Independent Broadcasting Authority)

Index

149